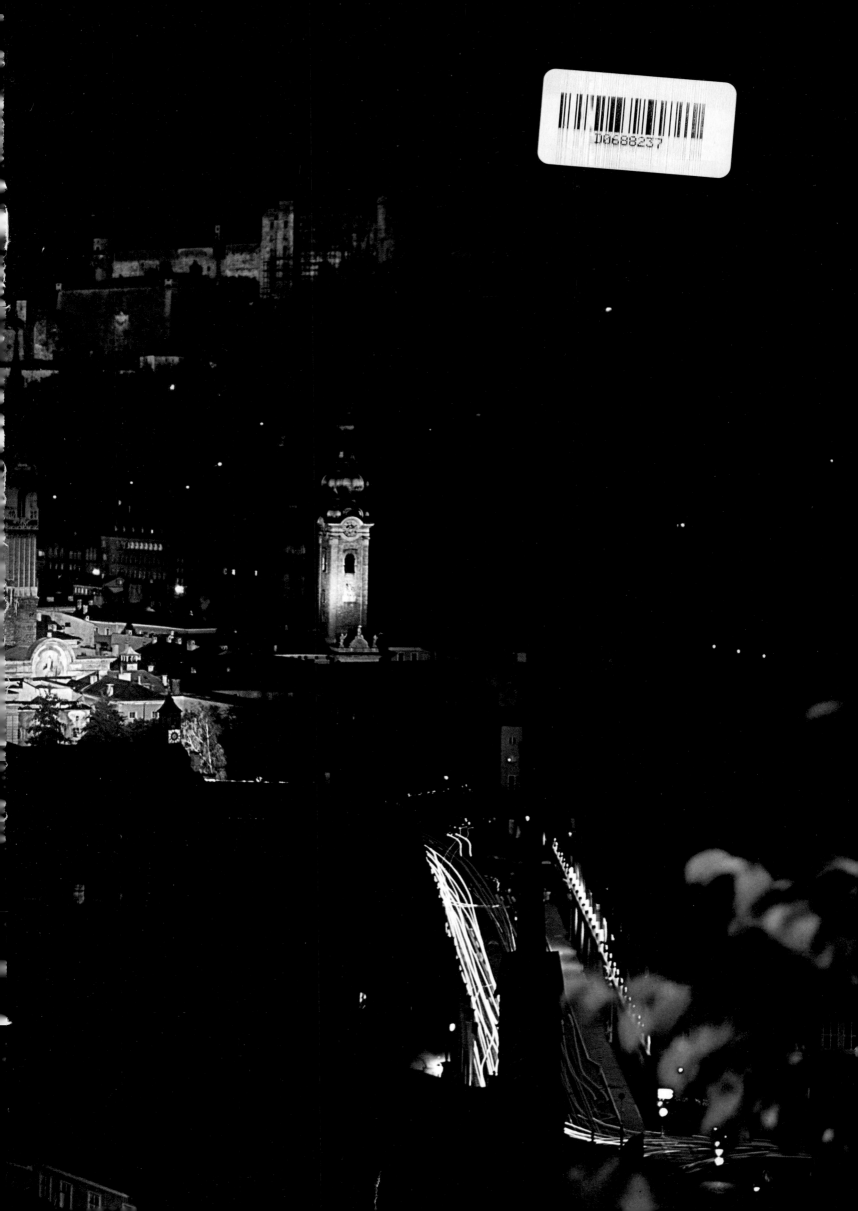

THE GREAT PLACES OF EUROPE

Text by
LIA PIEROTTI CEI

Translated by
Godfrey Ivins

LIBER

THE SKELLIGS AND CHRIST'S SADDLE

In order to gather his thoughts, meditate or make an act of faith, man has always sought the solitude of some lofty, inaccessible peak, from which his prayers might soar more easily heavenwards. A number of monasteries, abbeys and hermitages, • apparently suspended in mid-air, compel the admiration of the traveler, who can barely imagine how such feats can have been accomplished at a time when the builders had little but their hands to rely on and would often spend an entire lifetime at work on a single site. Yet, whether they were rich or poor, powerful lords or lowly peasants, priests or laymen, the spiritual force which drove them on was strong enough to overcome the limitations of nature and impose on them a superior will.

The remains which can be seen to this day on the Skellig Islands, off the coast of County Kerry, in the southwest corner of Ireland, make an unforgettable sight. Lemon Rock and the two Skellig Islands themselves seem to rise out the ocean, their sheer faces towering more than six hundred feet above the waves. It was here, cut off from the world for much of the year by fog and storms, that the first Christians withdrew to do penance. All that remains of their monastery is the ruins of two churches (St. Michael's, the larger of the two, dating from after the year 1000, while the other is doubtless of earlier origin), of two oratories and six cells, as well as a cemetery. For centuries on end pilgrims journeyed there, braving the fury of the sea in their frail boats, in order to climb barefoot up the narrow paths which lead to the top of the island—known, on account of its peculiar shape, as Christ's Saddle. It is no longer possible to make out the names of the monks

carved on the stone. Each spring, without regard for the weight of years or the anger of sky and waves, nature spreads a mantle of greenery over the ruins, in which the birds living among the bushes welcome the return of the sun at dawn each day. Yet one cannot help pondering on the lives of those men, dedicated as they were by profound faith and mysticism, to contemplation and prayer.

The Skelling Islands, in the southwest corner of Ireland: interesting remains of Celtic structures used by the first Irish Christians.

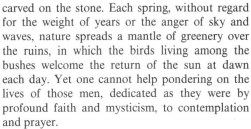

THE MYSTERY OF STONEHENGE

If we look up the word "Stonehenge", the encyclopedia tells us that it is the site, about eight miles from Salisbury, of the mysterious remains of one of the biggest megalithic monuments built in prehistoric times during the transition from the Neolithic to the Bronze Age about 4,000 years ago. "Megalith" means "large stone": the object of our interest is a complex built of huge blocks of sandstone.

According to the archaelogists, Stonehenge was built in several stages, each lasting several centuries, and served as a place of worship for the Druids. Slabs of stone fixed vertically in the ground are known as *menhirs,* and menhirs covered by a horizontal stone form a *dolmen.* Together, menhirs and dolmens make a *cromlech,* a group of giants, silent guardians of secrets which the visitor dares not intrude on.

Stonehenge is difficult to describe: it consists of blocks of sarsen stone (the word is cognate with "Saracen"), originally one hundred of them 30 feet tall together with some smaller blocks of bluestone arranged in a horseshoe shape, forming two concentric circles and two ellipses, surmounted by rectangular stones which form a continuous architrave. Within the circles stand five enormous dolmens formed by ten menhirs joined up in pairs by an architrave and known as *trilithons.* In the center is an altar, at the entrance is the sacrificial stone and in the middle of the outside avenue is the *Heel Stone,* a menhir whose significance is uncertain.

Probably Stonehenge is something quite different from the monument perceived by official archaeology. Ten years ago G.S. Hawkins, an American astronomer born in England, visited the site and carefully examined the ground plan, the surroundings, including the tumuli, wells and the monument known as the Sanctuary.

After his visit Hawkins was not convinced by the orthodox view of the site. He researched, calculated, reflected and finally came to the conclusion that Stonehenge was neither a sacrifical temple nor one dedicated to the Sun God: it was in fact an observatory.

It was well known that at the summer solstice the sun could be seen to rise over the Heel Stone: was that pure chance or the result of human design?

Stonehenge certainly had a precise purpose, like many other megalithic monuments, but it is still not certain what this purpose was. Prehistoric man is thought to have had a very primitive level of civilisation, and we find it difficult to understand how the men of 4,000 years ago managed to cut and square the stone so accurately by hand, lift and place the sandstone blocks weighing 25 tons and transport bluestone weighing five tons from a quarry 240 miles away.

Whilst we hope that this fascinating enigma will one day be explained, we must for the present be content to admire with astonishment and curiosity the work of men who, long ago, were probably studying the sky to find an answer to the mystery of our existence.

Two views of the Stonehenge megaliths. There are several different hypotheses as two the origin of this impressive monumental arrangement of stone blocks.

LONDON, THE HOUSES OF PARLIAMENT

Everybody knows London's Houses of Parliament, at least by hearsay or in their imagination. And here they are in front of us now, in all their grandeur, evoking all the historic events and famous names that have gone to make the history of England.

They stand in Parliament Square, one façade reflected in the quiet waters of the Thames and the other flanked by Westminster Abbey.

They are a splendid group of buildings in pure perpendicular Gothic, bristling with turrets and spires, and at either end stand two famous towers: the Victoria Tower, 102 meters high, and the clock tower, 96 meters high, containing the most famous bell and chimes in the world, Big Ben. Londoners are so proud of the accuracy of Big Ben's clock that they say that to correct the balance of its mechanism you only need to use a halfpenny piece.

The origins of the Houses of Parliament go back to a royal palace built around the 11th century. In subsequent centuries it was rebuilt, extended and then abandoned at the time of Henry VIII. In 1547 Edward VI made this the

permanent seat of Parliament.

The buildings we see today are rather more recent, built in fact between 1840 and 1852 according to the plans drawn up by Sir Charles Barry and Augustus Pugin, replacing buildings which had been destroyed by fire in 1834.

The sheer scale and beauty of the exterior are equalled by the interest of the interior, parts of which symbolise English tradition and democracy. Westminster Hall, for example, is a huge hall dating from the 13th century which until 1882 housed the Courts of Justice: it is 72 meters long, 20 wide and 27 high, and it is lit by double and multi-arched windows which cast mysterious and changing shadows over its roof of vast oak beams, built in 1399 and considered to be amongst the oldest in the world.

Other, and not less famous, parts of this complex are the House of Lords, with its twelve fine windows and rich frescoes, and the House of Commons, rebuilt in pure Gothic style by Gilbert Scott in 1950.

When Parliament is sitting late into the night a lamp shines from the clock tower. When the House of Commons is in daytime session a flag flies from the Victoria Tower.

London: Big Ben and the Houses of Parliament, the symbol of democracy.

FOR EACH TRUTH
THERE ARE MANY LIES

The "many lies" are the portraits of an actual historical personage who has the ability to dig down into the human soul and uncover the most hidden motives and dramatic, twisted, morbid, malicious or bitter passions.

As we are now at Stratford-on-Avon it is obvious that are speaking of William Shakespeare, born in 1564 in this town in the county of Warwickshire and on the left bank of the River Avon.

Stratford has its roots in the distant past. Towards the end of the twelfth century it began to flourish under Bishop John of Coutances on a site which had been occupied in the days of the Romans.

Set in green, wooded countryside, the town's chief attractions are the house where Shakespeare was born and the performances of his plays at the fine theater. Stratford has retained many of its old buildings, the river flows past verdant banks and meadows, and the pace of life quickens only on market days and at fair time. The most important is Mop Fair in October, when marvellous roast beef and pork delight the palates of local gourmets. They and everyone else feel obliged to pay their respects at the tomb of Stratford's most famous citizen in Holy Trinity Church, stop a moment before his monument with its colored bust and wonder about him and his works.

Like many other Stratford buildings, the modest house in Henley Street is half-timbered and shows its wooden framework quite clearly. Declared a national monument in 1847, it houses a museum and a library with some fine and rare collections.

Its walls still seem to throb with life. Amongst the most impressive features of the place, besides the cradle and the big stone fireplaces, is the garden, which contains all the trees and flowers mentioned in Shakespeare's works. The Shakespeare Memorial Theater is an important part of Stratford. Every year there are festivals and commemorations of all kinds. The theater, rebuilt in 1929 and 1932 after a fire, is equipped with the very latest in stage machinery. The library and the gallery contain a wealth of relics, the most interesting of which is a collection of portraits executed by a multitude of great artists, including that by Droeshout. Perhaps that is his true likeness?

In reality a man like William Shakespeare can present a different face to each of his devotees, the face each thinks he perceives from the works. After all, they are his supreme artistic creation: "the rest is silence".

Stratford-on-Avon: left and facing, Shakespeare's house and Anne Hathaway's cottage; above and right, two views of the Shakespeare Memorial Theatre.

HELSINGÖR, OR RATHER "ELSINORE"

Helsingör is about 40 kilometers north of Copenhagen, the capital of Denmark, situated on the island of Sjaelland opposite the Swedish city of Hälsingborg, but everyone knows it better as "Elsinore", for this is Shakespeare's name for the castle of Kronborg situated to the north of the city.

The Shakespearian hero who murmurs "To be or not to be" while wandering deeply troubled in mind on the walls of this imposing castle, is an imaginary person, for the real Hamlet ("Amled" in Danish) was a Viking who lived several centuries before Kronborg castle was built.

Built in Dutch Renaissance style between 1574 and 1585 for King Frederick II by the architects Hans Paascke and Antonius Opbergen, it was restored from 1635 to 1640 and considered at the time to be an impregnable fortress, one of the most secure in Europe. The Danes were confident that its stout bastions, five towers and wide ditches would repel all attackers. However, in 1658 Kronberg was taken by the Swedes, who destroyed the beautiful fountain in its courtyard, the work of G. van der Schardt. In 1629 a terrible fire gutted most of the interior of the castle. The chronicles of the time tell us that the great Hall of the Knights was hung with magnificent tapestries which Hans Knieper, a great master of his art, made for Frederick II. They portrayed the hundred and eleven kings of Denmark who had preceded him. Fortunately part of them can still be seen in the National Museum in Copenhagen. But if you want to see the canopy of the royal throne you will have to go to Stockholm, where it has been since 1658, when the Swedes captured the castle.

In one wing of the castle the chapel has been recently restored; little remains of the

original structure, which dates back to the 15th century, whilst the altarpiece dates back to 1587.

Despite sacking, fire and the weather, Kronborg still retains all its drama and fascination. Austere, mysterious, it both attracts and disturbs the visitor with its well-kept gardens, tall trees and view of the sea in the distance, where only four kilometers of water separate Denmark from Sweden.

On stormy nights, when lamplight pierces the darkness, it is not difficult to imagine, as Shakespeare did, the ghost of the dead King of Denmark haunting the battlements of the castle of Elsinore.

Four photographs of Kronbourg Castle, at Elsinore: Hamlet's castle.

OLD LADIES LOOKING IN THE MIRROR

In Amsterdam, in the calm waters of the Prinsengracht (the canal named after the Prince of Orange) you can see the reflections of the façades of delightful old houses. They have something of the coquetry of aristocratic old ladies who continue to admire themselves in the mirror, despite their wrinkles.

No other Dutch city can boast of such a wide variety of harmonious buildings and historical monuments. Their images are reflected in the changing surface of the water and vary according to the time of day and one's position in the most intriguing way.

At the point where the Prinsengracht joins the historic center of Amsterdam the view of the canal seems like a composition in watercolor with the typical tonality of a Dutch picture incorporating the history of its greatest works of art, especially Rembrandt's paintings.

Born in Leyden on 15th July 1606, son of Harmen Gerrits-zoon van Rijn, a prosperous miller, Rembrandt showed precocious genius. When he was fourteen he matriculated as a student in the Faculty of Letters of the famous University of Leyden, and while studying he used to visit the studio of the painter Jacob van Swanemburg. Three years later he moved to Amsterdam, where he studied under Pieter Lastiman, an artist who in his travels in Italy had absorbed some of the ideas of painters such as Caravaggio.

In 1624 Rembrandt returned to his birthplace and began a period of hard work which produced many drawings, portraits, self-portraits and biblical compositions. For these his models were his friends and acquaintances, the poor, the unhappy and the old, of whom he studied and absorbed every detail and every nuance of feeling. And because he was young he delighted in transferring his youth to canvas, together with the sumptuous folds of the drapery, the whiteness of the collars, the richness of the jewels and the sensuousness of the women.

At the age of 25, in 1631, Rembrandt moved back to Amsterdam, where he moved into a house in the Jodenbreestraat which was to be his home until 1660. Nowadays it can still be seen with its flight of four steps and typical red shutters, but it is now a museum, containing many of his works. His greatest paintings, such as the celebrated *Night Watch*, can be seen at the Rijksmuseum, and other works are in the greatest galleries in the world.

Not much is known of Rembrandt's life. Apart from his artistic achievements we know of his happy marriage in 1634 to Saskia van Uylenburch, who was his principal model for various canvases, his children, most of whom died early, his later marriage to young Hendrickye Stoffels which lasted until his death. It is said that the great artist was a shy, unsociable, avaricious man of little culture. True or otherwise, it does not greatly matter. His message, his spiritual testament is with us still in the many faces of suffering, tired, sad, anxious or happy humanity he saw and put down on his canvases with brush strokes rich in contrastive effects. Thus all speaks unmistakably of him, his lowlands and mills, his light-effects and shadows of passing clouds, his bridges which span the canals of Amsterdam to meet at the Westerkerk, where in October 1669 he was buried.

Left, exterior and interior of Rembrandt's house; right, one of the many canals which give Amsterdam its unique charm.

THE CONTRADICTIONS
OF THE GRAND'PLACE

The Grand'Place, the famous square in Brussels which is the heart of the Belgian capital, delights the spectator with its harmony, its historical importance and its architectural inventiveness.

The eye of the beholder runs over the four sides this great rectangle (360 feet by 225), in which fine houses from different periods are aligned and fused together by one common source of inspiration, the Renaissance. Italianate elements are mixed with lively Flemish imagination which enlivens the sobriety of the buildings with exciting use of profile, ornamentation, statues and small columns. But this architectural balance and elegance was in days gone by the scene of violence and profound hatred. The lively flower market which nowadays brightens up the square, cannot blot out the memory of the terrifying events of 1558, when Counts Egmont and Horn were beheaded in the Spanish reaction led by the Duke of Alba. But everything repeats itself in the pages of human history: Truth and Falsehood, Discord and Peace are symbolised by the statues below the top storey of the "Maison du Louvre", at Number 5, the work of the sculptor Marcus De Vos, which serves to remind one of these contradictions. And perhaps Victor Hugo thought of his "Miserables" when looking out from his house ("Le Pigeon", Number 26) at the great relief of Abundance on the pediment of the magnificent Palace of the Dukes of Brabant (1698).

There is the Hôtel de Ville, the most famous Town Hall in Belgium, the oldest and most Gothic of Gothic secular buildings. Built at various times, begun in 1402, altered, burned down, rebuilt and restored on the course of centuries, this building has suffered more than any other from the vicissitudes of time and the differing solutions of a long succession of architects, each with new ideas, adding new wings, new façades, fountains, spires and statues.

Number 9, the Maison du Cygne (1698), and Number 10, the Maison des Brasseurs (seventeenth century), surmounted by the equestrian statue of Charles of Lorraine (1854), seem to demonstrate the passing of the centuries and the tyranny of time (inside the palace is an interesting museum devoted to the history of brewing). Then there is the "Maison de la Balance" with negro caryatids (1704) which underlines another contradiction: the balance, symbol of justice and the negro, symbol of slavery.

One's eyes turn to the other buildings, eager to see and to appraise them: the "Maison des Tailleurs", "du Paon", "du Chêne" but here is the most famous house of all: the "Maison du Roi" whose misleading name seems to indicate a royal residence but designates nothing more than a bread-shop. Beginning life as a bakery, it was rebuilt by Keldermans the Younger at the command of the Emperor Charles V (1512) and entirely restored in 1873. It now houses a local historical museum.

But already night is falling: the outlines of the buildings stand out against the violet sky and then fade away altogether. The lights come on and we see a great blaze of lights, a varied and compelling scene, a festive atmosphere, in which the contrast between ancient and modern adds to the impact of the wonderful Grand'Place.

Brussels: the Grand'Place, by night and day, and its famous Hôtel-de-Ville. Lower left, details of the Renaissance façades.

BRUGES: RELIGION AND TRADE

Bruges (or Brugge) is called the Venice of the North. The comparison springs easily to one's mind, for the two cities have many affinities: a network of canals, their air of serenity, hump-backed bridges, quiet wharves alongside ancient houses mirrored in the sluggish waters, love of art, high standard of craftmanship in lace-making, a historical inheritance and a common fate. Nowadays people say Venice is dying, and in the twelfth century they were saying the same about Bruges. One French author has called it *"Bruges-la-morte"* or "Dead Bruges".

Bruges has preserved its mediaeval character intact. The Beguinage is an intriguing feature of the city. It was founded in 1245 by Margaret, Countess of Flanders and Princess of Constantinople, and stands in a quiet little square. The main buildings, the Begijnhof, which seems to invite meditation and prayer, has a lovely eighteenth-century entrance which leads to the site's historical museum. Number 30 is the former house of the Superiors. To the south lies the famous Minnesee, or "Lake of Love", a must for every tourist.

The mystical atmosphere which permeates Bruges is to be found not only in its churches but also in its peaceful, tree-lined streets and picturesque corners in soft watercolor tints. Its roots lie in the deep religious fervor of the twelfth and thirteenth centuries. From this period come the Cathedral of the Holy Savior (the oldest Gothic church in the region, with many masterpieces of Flemish art), the Church of Our Lady with its

16

huge tower, built in various stages after 1210, the Church of St. Jacob, a Gothic church started in 1180 and not finished until 1457-78, containing many works of art. Almost as if to counterbalance the religious fervor, there was an equally intense commercial activity. Bruges' nearness to the sea, the suitability of the Zwyn estuary for navigation and hence for seaborne trade, these are the factors which enabled Bruges to compete with great maritime trading cities like Venice and Genoa. In partnership with Arab and Syrian merchants it extended its trade to the Middle East. The mid-fourteenth and fifteenth centuries saw Bruges at the peak of its splendor, having 80 guilds and industries producing many luxury goods. But the discovery of America, the silting-up of the Zwyn, the decline of the wool trade and the rise of the port of Antwerp spelled its doom. Nowadays the city is recovering its prosperity, partly because of the opening of a canal linking it with the sea and partly because of the growth of tourism.

Bruges' remarkable museums have some outstanding paintings, including some by Jan van Eyck and Hans Memling, and famous sculptures such as Michelangelo's *Madonna with Child* in the Vrouwekerk. There is also the fine, wide Market Square, a synthesis of its ancient greatness and a living testimony to its splendor.

Left, two views of Bruges, the "Venice of the North". Right and above, the City Gate and the Hôtel-de-Ville.

A POET FOR A CATHEDRAL

If you are in a hurry, don't go into Notre Dame, for there are too many things to see and take in. If you are not, have a look at the left-hand portal, and you will see Maurice de Sully offering the plan of his church to the Blessed Virgin. It is the year 1163, the year in which the construction of the cathedral on the Ile de la Cité started, in that holy place *par excellence* where there had been a Gallic temple, then a Roman one (there are some remains of it in the Musée de Cluny) which became a chapel dedicated to the Virgin and was then burned down by the Vikings in the ninth century.

The bishop's plan was ambitious. He wanted a huge cathedral built to precise plans. History does not relate who the original architects were; they might well have been humble masons working under the direction of Maurice de Sully, who had large resources and funds at his disposal.

After the death of Bishop Maurice in 1196 the choir was finished, but another 75 years went by before the rest was completed.

Artists famous and unknown enriched it with their works, filling it with a crowd of madonnas, saints, prophets, virgins wise and foolish, fantastic monsters, ordinary folk and wandering scholars.

Considered one of the oldest Gothic cathedrals in France, (though work done on it over the centuries has left traces of a whole range of architectural styles), Notre Dame suffered greatly during the French Revolution. The credit for its subsequent restoration is largely due to Victor Hugo, who in his historical novel *Notre Dame* denounced the profanation and misuse to which the architectural masterpiece of the past had been subjected. In a series of dramatic questions the poet put the blame on public opinion and demanded that the public pay more attention to restoring the monuments of the past and repairing

the damage caused by the violence or uncultured stupidity of mankind.

The "queen of cathedrals", as Hugo calls it, towers over the center of Paris in all its solemn splendor. Its façade is thought to be one of the best and noblest expressions of Gothic art, due mainly to its three Gothic-arched doors, its 28 royal niches surrounded by an indented string course, its huge central Rose-window and the gallery of slender columns above which its two massive, harmonious towers rise up into the sky.

Just as fascinating are the south façade with its flying buttresses (a technical feat of Gothic architecture), the spacious windows with a pillar on either side, the transept with its two Rose-windows one above the other and the slender spire pointing up to the heavens.

The interior offers the spectator a whole series of delights: the nave is a mixture of Romanesque and early Gothic, 75 columns support vaults 115 feet above ground level. From the

gallery of the triforium you have a marvellous view of the choir, but some of the choicest masterpieces are the huge thirteenth-century Rose-windows. Their sections of colored glass set in lead cast fantastic pools of colored light.

The cathedral has an enormously rich treasury which still receives gifts from all over the world. Notre Dame has been the scene of many historic events, royal weddings and coronations, the most famous of which was that of Napoléon when he became Emperor of the French. The most curious one was the occasion of the wedding of Charles VI to Isabella of Bavaria in 1385, when a tightrope-walker came down a cord attached to the top of one of the two towers to crown the new queen of France.

Notre-Dame de Paris: one of its marvellous stained-glass windows; the sanctuary, seen from the banks of the Seine, and the apse seen from outside.

VERSAILLES

Occasionally the most daring or most important works, the most courageous or even reckless enterprises come about almost by chance, as a result of the desire to imitate or excel. This is precisely the origin of the Palace of Versailles, the regal and enduring monument to Louis XIV, known to history as the "Sun King". Versailles also symbolises the might of the French monarchy, which in its prime dominated political events in Europe.

Nicolas Fouquet, Intendant of Finances, built himself a magnificent château just outside Paris. In 1661 Louis, then only 23, visited it when he was guest of honor at a banquet given by Fouquet for 6000 guests and was amazed. That evening Louis had an urgent and overwhelming desire to build a place even more splendid than Fouquet's. He chose as his site Versailles, where he already had a small château or hunting lodge.

Circumstances favored the king, for not long afterwards Fouquet was condemned to life imprisonment for treason and embezzlement. Louis confiscated all Fouquet's works of art and then engaged Le Vau, formerly Fouquet's architect and a man of proven ability and imagination.

For ever after the king was in the grip of a building craze. To the existing building at Versailles he added the great Cour Royale and the Place d'Armes with its stables large and small, the work of Jules Hardouin Mansart, another famous architect. Behind the palace the master gardener Le Nôtre created beautiful formal gardens in the French manner, containing flowers of every kind, pools, bushes and trees. Special importance was given to the Orangery, for orange trees were the king's special favorites.

Fountains, statues, marble courtyards,

king chose as his personal emblem, thus becoming the "Sun King".

Splendid as the exterior of Versailles looks, its interior is equally beautiful: the long staircase with its hundred steps, the Queen's Staircase, the Royal Chapel, the famous Hall of Mirrors (built in 1678 and lit by as many as three thousand candles on state occasions) with its 17 tall windows looking out over the park and its 17 matching mirrors on the opposite wall, the King's Bedchamber, the Queen's Bedchamber, the Dauphin's Library and the Galerie des Batailles.

Those who love statistics will be interested to know that the head gardener used almost two million flower-pots to grow the infinite variety of flowers and other plants which flourished in the greenhouses, and that almost 35,000 workmen of all kinds were employed in the building of the Versailles complex. At the end of the 17th century there were 1400 fountains in the gardens of Versailles.

After the French Revolution Versailles fell into neglect, then became a museum and was partly restored in the early 1900's in a manner which enables us to see the sometimes extravagant signs of past splendors: pictures, tapestries, carpets, statues, clocks, furniture, all these tell the story of an age of incredible pomp and the desire of one man to show the world the economic and artistic strength of his country and his own greatness.

Versailles: left, the Galerie des Glaces and the Petit Trianon; on this page, the ornate wrought-iron grill, the château seen from the ponds, the gardens and the main courtyard with the statue of Louis XIV.

gilding, friezes, balustrades, roofs of gleaming slate, even a menagerie with birds and animals of every kind: thus Versailles was continually extended and embellished at the command of the insatiable Louis. In the park behind the palace he built the Grand Trianon with its elegant colonnade, the Petit Trianon with its belvedere, the Temple of Love and the Grotto of Thetis, the finest work of all, surmounted by its Apollo medallion. This symbol of the Greek Sun God the

MONT-SAINT-MICHEL
AU PERIL DE LA MER

For every place there is a time of day which is more evocative than any other. Sometimes it is dawn, or sunset or midday, when the sun puts shadow to flight, or the night of the full moon.

Mont-Saint-Michel, the abbey-fortress which stands on the island of the same name off the coast between Normandy and Brittany, is one of the most interesting examples of French mediaeval monastic architecture, and it should best be seen before sunrise, when the sky is changing color and when the pale light of dawn dims the brilliance of the stars. The light mist thins out and gradually a fantastic castle appears, magnificent and imposing to the eye of the observer. Bastions and buttresses stoutly built in stone seem to rise gradually towards the sky against which are outlined battlements and pinnacles. At the highest point stands a gothic spire bearing the figure of St. Michael the Archangel with outstretched sword.

It is said that many centuries ago this very rock, surrounded by thick forests, was chosen by the Druids as the site of their rituals. Later the Romans built a simple temple and named the island Jupiter's Mount. Several centuries later the rock was occupied by Christian hermits. In the year 708 the Bishop of Avranches dedicated it to St. Michael, who, it is said, had appeared to him and ordered him to construct a chapel in that place. In 966 Richard I, Duke of Normandy, founded there a monastery for a group of Italian monks from the abbey of Monte Casino. The church rapidly became a center of attraction, and many pilgrims helped to enrich it by their offerings.

At the outbreak of the Hundred Years War the rock was so well fortified that the English were unable to take it. Both the abbey and the fortress, extended and embellished in the course of centuries, became more and more fascinating.

The Early Romanic style which is to be seen in its columns and arches is mingled with flamboyant Gothic. The Abbey is a labyrinth of rooms, angles, niches and staircases. These lead from the monks, quarters in a mediaeval building called "la Merveille" to the "Lace Staircase", a masterpiece of fretted stone by which one can reach the top of the choir.

Equally delightful is the cloister, also a masterpiece of French Gothic. The arcade which surrounds it has a double row of slender, elegant columns with sculptured capitals.

This heavily fortified citadel was for several centuries a grim prison. Though it was formerly joined to the mainland, in the course of the centuries Mont-Saint-Michel has become separated from it when the tide comes in. The tide is one of the highest in the world and its rise makes an extremely interesting spectacle. Indeed it is the waves of the swiftly advancing sea which have given the place the name *"Mont-Saint-Michel au péril de la mer"*.

Aerial views of the abbey of Mont-Saint-Michel, a unique gem of the Middle Ages.

CHARTRES—THE CATHEDRAL

The destination of a constant stream of pilgrims, this church dedicated to the Holy Virgin is justly considered by many to be the most beautiful ecclesiastical building of the Middle Ages and the epitome of the French Gothic.

Built originally in the Romanesque style by St. Fulbert during the first half of the year 1000, soon afterwards it was devastated by fire; not even the new building built in 1194 was spared by the flames, although fortunately it was not completely destroyed.

Year after year, century after century, the cathedral, rebuilt in the Gothic style but preserving some of the Romanesque elements, was enriched by the addition of chapels, porticoes, towers: the Portico of the Kings (1145-1155) with the three great windows, the topless spire, straight as an arrow against the sky, the Clock Pavillion, the beautiful statue-pillars representing prophets and biblical characters, the choir surrounded by a rich circle of sculptures. But of all the beauties of this cathedral—meant to be contemplated without haste and to be discovered in silence and solitude as if they were pages from the Gospels—there are two which above all others are supremely magical and impressive: the seemingly endless series of arches between tall circular or polygonal pillars that spread the whole length of the building in a marvellous play of curves like bold paintstrokes, and the lofty stained glass windows, amongst the

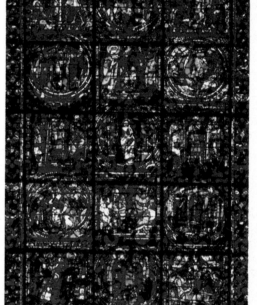

most famous in the world.

How can one resist standing filled with speechless admiration in front of these: the three windows in the main façade which portray the life and passion of Christ, the image of Our Lady of the Belle Verrière, the rose-windows, the colored medallions which commemorate saints, members of the guilds, generous benefactors?

These stained glass windows are a real miracle, for during the rebuilding of the cathedral they were made with miraculous speed. Even more miraculous is the fact that they survived the French Revolution and the Second World War. However, in 1792 the cathedral suffered great damage and the contents of its Treasury were lost.

A fortunate accident? It might be better to believe in the power of faith.

The cathedral of Chartres: interior, side door and detail of the façade, with the remarkable rose window.

A CHATEAU TO DREAM ABOUT

Many European châteaux and castles are built on the ruins of older fortresses, often retaining the defense potential, sometimes playing the role of showplace, holiday-spot, or hideaway. Emperors and kings, nobles, court favorites have at least one, surrounded by parks, lovely gardens, sparkling fountains and cages filled with gaily-colored birds. Within are rooms and salons embellished by tapestries, elegant furniture, carpets, pictures, sculptures, china signed by the finest artists of the age, collected to beautify a residence already magnificent, to arouse the envy of friends and enemies and to demonstrate to the world the good taste and power of its owner.

Chambord, about eight miles from Blois, is certainly the most harmonius Renaissance château in France. It was built on the site of a medieval fortress, retaining the latter's solid, square structure, with sides 510 feet long and a height of 384 feet.

Begun by François I in 1519, the central section of the château was completed with five round towers with pointed roofs, whilst the keep, which stands to one side, has four smaller towers. The terraces, completed in 1532, are surmonted by spires, gables, small bell-towers and airy pinnacles which make the château not only imposing but even like something from a fairy-

Two views of the Château de Chambord and its famous twin spiral stairways.

tale, like a picture painted by a medieval miniaturist.

Chambord is also famous for its staircases. The most famous is a beautiful one with a double spiral, so that visitors can go up and down it at the same time without coming face-to-face. Originally the staircase consisted of just one flight, detached from the main body of the building and projecting boldly as far as the terrace of the great tower. The landings have been added later, perhaps for convenience or safety, but they break the harmony of the proportions and spoil that sense of upward striving which the design possesses.

As you walk through the two floors of the galleries, take a look through the lovely view. The countryside round about and the magnificent rolling parkland extends over 13,000 acres and is bounded by a wall nearly 20 miles long.

Other French châteaux share this pleasing characteristic with Chambord, and their well-proportioned lines are models which prevailed for another two centuries despite the extreme indulgence in ornamentation which preceded the Baroque.

Chambord was one of the favorite residences of Louis XIV, of Stanislas Leszcynsky and the Maréchal de Saxe, to whom it was given by Louis XV. Later it was presented to Henri de Bourbon by national subscription. In 1932 the house of Bourbon-Parma transferred the ownership from Henri, duc de Chambord, to the French state.

THE PALACES OF FREDERICK THE GREAT

Frederick II, King of Prussia, was rightly called "Great"; his talents were not in fact only military, capable though they were of defeating the Austrians under Charles of Lorraine, fighting on the side of the British and laying the foundations of the future military might of Prussia.

His father, Frederick William I, King of Prussia from 1713 to 1740, was nicknamed the *Sergeant King*. A sergeant who has enough ability can indeed become a head of state, but a head of state who deserves the nickname *Sergeant* must surely lack the qualities necessary for governing a kingdom wisely.

Frederick William I hated culture and was extremely tight-fisted as well, so that after his death he left behind a full treasury. He possessed a certain power of intuition in military affairs which made him, if not a good soldier, at least a moderately competent strategist. In 1715 he drove the Swedes out of Stralsund and in 1717 abolished the political power of his feudal vassals. Totally uncultivated himself, he so despised men of letters that he appointed a lunatic as president of the Berlin Academy.

His son Frederick II, born in 1712, was quite different, probably as a conscious reaction against his father: enlightened, a patron and protector of literature, the arts and sciences, he encouraged trade and industry. Endowed with great artistic talent, he was also a lively and witty writer (his works include his *Antimachiavelli, Mémoires relating to the history of the House of Brandeburg* and a *Legal Code*). Passionately interested in philosophy, he made Voltaire an honored guest at his court.

Frederick loved beauty, whether it was the beauty of nature or the beauty created by human hands. That is why he chose Potsdam as his favorite residence and built there the palaces and other works which make up all that is most distinctive and characteristic in Prussian art.

Potsdam, situated in north-west Germany not far from Berlin, started as a trading center of Slav origin in about the tenth century. In 1300 it was granted civic status, but its real importance was decided by the rulers of Prussia, who chose it as their second capital.

Unfortunately World War II has damaged many of Frederick's churches, including the enormous Stadt-Schloss built towards the end of the seventeenth century and extended in the following century by G.W. von Knobelsdorff. The rococo decorations in Frederick's appartments are splendid. The Court Church built by Philip Gerlach between 1731 and 1735 and containing the tombs of Frederick the Great and his father Frederick William I, has also been partly destroyed.

Many magnificent buildings remain, however, including the summer palace of Sans Souci with its sober elegance of design, the pavilions, the Orangerie, the delightful park with its magnificent Japanese magnolias, the Marble Palace and the Garnisonskirche.

Potsdam, sited on its wooded hillside and brightened by the cool waters of the Havel, is today an important industrial center for engineering, textiles and precision tools and has a geophysical and astrophysical observatory.

Gallery, façade and gardens of the marvellous Château of Sanssouci, at Potsdam, a masterpiece of rococo art.

THE MAGNIFICENT REFUGE OF A REBEL MONK

About the year 1070 Landgraf Ludwig built the Wartburg on the slopes of the Thuringian Forest.

St. Elisabeth was a guest in this splendid if austere residence from 1113 to 1131. About 1200 the Landgraf Hermann made it a focal point for the activities of troubadours, who vied with each other in poetry and song in the great hall painted with frescoes by Moritz von Schindl.

Meanwhile the town of Eisenach grew up at the foot of the Wartburg. It was a pleasant and quiet place which in the course of time was embellished by fine houses and churches such as the Romanesque St. Nicholas, church and Dominican convent dating from 1235. The people of the town traded in agricultural products, produced stout wooden furniture, set up schools and took an interest in artistic and spiritual affairs.

And it was at Eisenach, between 1498 and 1501, that a certain fifteen-year-old completed his secondary school education, a youth who would soon overthrow the ancient traditions of the Catholic Church. His name was Martin Luther.

Born in Eisleben in Saxony in 1483, Martin was the son of a miner, his family and background being poor but intensely pious. He suffered a religious crisis whilst studying Law at the University of Erfurt, entered the Augustinian order, became a theologian and then in 1508 professor at the University of Wittenberg. A few years later Luther was sickened by the sale of indulgences ordered by Leo X in order to collect money for the war against the Turks and the rebuilding of St. Peter's. In Germany the sale was in the hands of the Dominicans and degenerated rapidly into a mere financial operation, so the disgusted Luther wrote 95 "theses" against indulgences and on 31st October 1517 nailed them to the door of Wittenberg Cathedral.

The Pope treated the matter at first as an outburst of rivalry between the Augustinians and the Dominicans, but soon realised that it could have grave consequences. Summoned to Rome, Luther cleared himself of the charge of heresy. Despite the intervention of his great friend, Frederick, Elector of Saxony, Luther would not retreat a step. Leo X then sent out a Bull of Excommunication which the rebel monk burned in the square of Wittenberg to the cheers of the crowd.

The Reformation had begun. In 1520 Luther published three works which were absolutely fundamental to his doctrines, and these soon brought the most eminent humanists over to his side. In many German cities grave disorders broke out. The Emperor Charles V, with the Pope's agreement, invited Luther to the Diet of Worms to attempt a reconciliation, but without success. Placed under the ban of the empire, Luther was kidnapped by order of Frederick of Saxony and carried off to safety in the castle of the Wartburg. There he stayed for a year, translating the New Testament into German. Then, feeling secure enough to continue his struggle without personal danger, he left the castle and three years later married Catherine Bora, an ex-nun, in a convent in Wittenberg.

In the Wartburg one can still see the austere room in which Luther translated the Bible, and it is worth taking a look at the chapel, whose vault is supported by a richly-decorated column, the Landgraf's staircase, St. Elisabeth's gallery, the fine armory and the fifteenth-century House of the Knights.

In Eisenach can be seen the house where Luther lived, a building with Late Gothic features which contains a collection of editions of the Bible and other religious works. It is also worthwhile to admire the fine mid-eighteenth century Great Hall of the castle, complete with furniture and porcelain.

In the footsteps of Martin Luther, at the Wartburg, near Eisenach. It was at this desk that he translated the Old Testament into German.

A THEATER TAILORMADE FOR A GENIUS

Bayreuth, lying between the Jura and the Franconian Forest, is first mentioned in historical documents in the twelfth century. It was ruled by counts, burgraves and margraves who tossed it about amongst themselves, destroying it and rebuilding it, making it more beautiful. It passed into French hands in 1807 after the Treaty of Tilsit, and in 1810 Napoleon ceded it to Bavaria.

At Bayreuth one can admire many works of art: the immense Gothic cathedral begun in 1438, the Church of the Order of St. George in the form of a Greek cross and the Church of the Hospital with a ceiling painted by Wunder, the winding ramp in the old castle (its nucleus dates back to the sixteenth century) which allowed the passage of wheeled vehicles, and the Great Hall of the new castle with fine Rococo decorations. Notable too are the equestrian statue of Christian Ernst, the margrave's castles sited around Bayreuth and the Hermitage begun in 1720, which has a music room in a rich Rococo style.

But palaces, monuments and churches are not enough. The German people has always loved music and has given the world immortal musical geniuses. So one is not surprised at the fact that Bayreuth has one of the most important buildings in the history of the theater, where some of the most important writers and singers of the age put on their works under the patronage of dukes and princes willing to put up with the caprices and tantrums of a bel canto diva or a famous pianist.

The Bayreuth Opera House was built from 1744 to 1748 in accordance with ideas which were very modern for the period, with a stage 100 feet deep and as large as the orchestra stalls. The interior was designed by Carlo Bibbiena, architect and famous stage designer, whilst the façade was carried out by St. Pierre. The richness of the ornamentation and the whole style of the place (an exquisite variation of the Italian Baroque), make it a magnificent and worthy setting for the nobility.

In 1871 Richard Wagner came to Bayreuth and built the Villa Wahnfried not far from the house in which Liszt was to die in 1886. By now famous, the composer had completed the most complex and ambitious of all his works, the tetralogy known as the *Ring of the Nibelungen.*

Now he wanted an opera house in which that great poem could be suitably interpreted, a place in which the acoustics and the scenery, the rigor of form and substance, emotion and impetus would be intimately connected. He wanted a stage far removed from the smoky, evil-smelling offices and dense traffic of great cities, in an attractive and solitary place, an opera house without vanity, in short, one of his very own.

Bayreuth was the most suitable place, but the negotiations were long and wearisome and it was difficult to raise the necessary funds. By selling a thousand shares, by collecting contributions from Wagnerians everywhere, particularly the banker Feustel, and thanks principally to the 200,000 talers given by Ludwig II of Bavaria, one of Wagner's most fervent supporters, in 1876 the Festspielhaus opened with a performance of the *Ring*.

The Festspielhaus stands on a hill to the north of the town. The huge interior consists of a sector of a circle in which the stalls ascend in steps and the boxes are gathered at the bottom. The orchestra is not visible, being sited almost under the stage in the so-called "mystic gulf", and everything contributes to create the atmosphere desired by the master, to help the spirit to rise to the level which only the works of a genius can attain.

Wagner is buried in the garden of his villa, in the place designated by him beneath a block of marble without either ornament or inscription. One of the principal attractions of a visit to Bayreuth is indeed the Wagnerian monuments, the villa, gardens, Festspielhaus and archives, which include numerous anecdotes, critical studies and biographies of the great composer. It suffices to say that a catalog of 1883 already listed 10,180 of them!

Bayreuth: the theater of Richard Wagner, the original scenery for which was designed by the composer himself. Below, view of the splendid Château of the Ermitage.

OLD, YET ETERNALLY YOUNG

It is more than 500 years old, the oldest in present-day Germany, and still considered one of the greatest in Europe. It is eternally young, kept so by the thousands of young people who come there from all over the world. The subject is the University of Heidelberg, founded in 1386 by the Counts Palatine, who in the fourteenth century chose Heidelberg as their residence.

The area where the town sprang up, now the site of the university, is beyond doubt the most attractive one in the whole of Baden-Württemberg, where the River Neckar flows through a valley so pleasant and green that it constitutes a tourist attraction in its own right.

The origins of Heidelberg probably go back to the Roman period, but more definite evidence of its existence is found in thirteenth-century chronicles. In those days the land belonged to the bishops of Worms, who had taken it from the Counts Palatine of the Rhine. In 1239 it was granted city status. Its university soon acquired great fame because of the great scholars who taught there. In 1556 Heidelberg became Calvinist by order of the Elector Frederick III, at a time when a rift appeared in Protestant theology between Calvin and Zwingli on the one hand and Luther on the other. Ursus and Olevianus, members of the Faculty of Theology, drew up the "Heidelberg Catechism", which is considered equal in importance to Luther's. But the choice of this new religious doctrine had grim conseqences: a trying time began for Heidelberg which lasted not only throughout the Thirty Years War but for the rest of the century. In 1803 it passed into the possession of the Grand Duchy of Baden.

Heidelberg has fine cultural monuments and buildings, the most outstanding of which are the Parish Church of the fifteenth century, the Church of the Jesuits, the seventeenth-century arsenal and stables and the Knight's House.

The most famous historical site is the Schloss, thought to be one of the most beautiful and best-known in all Germany, but half-destroyed by the French in 1689. The main façade of the mediaeval fortress can still be seen together with buildings in the Flemish-Italian style of the sixteenth century. The section of the Heidelberg Schloss built between 1601 and 1607 has a garden in the Italian style with hedges and shrubs cut in decorative shapes. The Palatine Museum has interesting collections, including archaeological finds. Even more noteworthy is the ancient University Library, containing precious manuscripts of all kinds, many of them illuminated.

As for the university itself, that ancient but perpetually young institution, it has had famous professors such as the chemist Bunsen (1811-1899), the discoverer of spectrum analysis, the physicist Helmholz, who discovered the laws of the conservation of energy, the physicist Lenard 1862-1947) who won the 1905 Nobel Prize for his discovery of X rays, the modern philosopher Jaspers, the main exponent of existentialism, and at the present time has many eminent chemists, physicists, mathematicians, philosophers and medical men.

The lecture theaters and quadrangles of the university, the narrow mediaeval streets, the cafés and snackbars are the meeting-places of many races where an astounding variety of languages can be heard. Here people attend folk music and folk-dancing festivals, wine festivals, firework displays or earnest discussions of important problems. But along the banks of the Neckar one is likelier to come across a blue-eyed young Teuton passionately embracing a dark-haired girl. Thus those who have difficulty in understanding each other's words communicate perfectly in the universal language of love.

Heidelberg, on the banks of the Nekar. Above, the famous Philosopher's Lane, a place where much original thinking has been generated over the centuries. Right, the castle, one of the most beautiful in Germany.

THE CITY OF THE MUSENHOF

Some places more than others are linked with historical or fictional personages who are identified with the place so much that they obscure its origins and political history.

One of those places is Weimar, formerly the capital of Thuringia and nowadays the capital of the province of the same name. It is about fifty miles from Leipzig on the left bank of the River Ilm. Weimar's history goes back a thousand years, indeed there are even some traces of Roman occupation.

In the course of time this fine German town has been enriched with many churches, the most interesting of which is the Collegiate Church in the Late Gothic style, containing amongst other works of art a triptych by Lucas Cranach the Elder, who was buried in this very church. In the Schlossmuseum we can admire collections of paintings and sculptures of outstanding interest, and in the Museum of Prehistory we can see relics of the distant past, whilst the Palace of the Resistance is worthy of attention not only because of its importance but also because it was rebuilt under the direction of Goethe.

Goethe: that is one of the names with which Weimar is identified, together with Schiller, Liszt and the Duchess Anna Amalia who during her reign built the *Musenhof,* or Court of the Muses. From that period until the first half of the nineteenth century, when Goethe and Schiller moved there, Weimar was considered the cultural and spiritual center of Germany. From 1791 to 1817 the author of *Faust* was the director of the *Hoftheater* (Court Theater), quickly making it a

byword for exemplary, perfectionist, classical performances.

Weimar's artistic activity was for a short time reduced by the Napoleonic Wars. The French occupied it several times, but it soon recovered and regained its importance in the eyes of European artists and intellectuals. In 1848 Duke Karl Alexander appointed Franz Liszt as theater director. He produced *Tannhäuser* and later the première of *Lohengrin* which brought fame to Wagner.

Though Schiller died in 1805 and Goethe in 1832, their presence and influence can still be felt, and not only in the houses they lived in. They live on in the immortal masterpieces which these, the two greatest German poets, have left us and which Weimar inspired and applauded.

A monument to Goethe and Schiller stands in front of the Nationaltheater in Weimar. It shows them standing together on the same plinth and dedicates them to history: two friends, two poets, one and the same glory.

Weimar: above, Schiller's house; left, the Bürgerhaus; right, Goethe's house, his collections of antiques and the venerable table at which he worked.

big as swimming-pools. One of them was used for washing the archbishop's horses, more than a hundred of them.

Not far from Salzburg are the gardens of Hellbrunn, the summer palace built by Archbishop Marco Sittico, a successor of von Raitenau and a kinsman of the Medicis. Its fountains are masterpieces of hydraulic engineering: there we see the tiny inhabitants of a miniature town move about and perform amusing antics, whilst magic flutes sound from behind the trees.

Salzburg, a Mecca for music-lovers. Left: the house in which Mozart was born. It is now a museum dealing with his life and work, and, for music-lovers, an essential place to visit.

SALZBURG, THE CITY OF THE "MAGIC FLUTE"

If you want to find real happiness, you must visit Salzburg. This little Austrian town in the midst of snow-covered mountains produces a strange euphoria in you, almost as if the sound of Pamino's flute or Mozart's immortal music still echoed within its walls.

The Hohensalzburg fortress dominates the city and stands out boldly against the sky. Lower down we see Salzburg's magnificent cathedral with its two towers. All around you are colorful churches, beautiful squares, over there the great clock.

The first inhabitants of Salzburg were not artists but men who mined the wealth hidden in the rocks: iron, gold, copper, silver, emeralds, marble and salt. The little village became a busy commercial center, but soon the church assumed political power and the Archbishops of Salzburg became its absolute rulers, to dominate it for a

thousand years. Though they were frequently cruel, they did make the city more and more beautiful. At the end of the 16th century Archbishop von Raitenau employed the Italian Pietro Scamozzi, already famous for the *Procuratie Nuovo* in St. Mark's Square, Venice. His brief was to build a cathedral even bigger than St. Peter's in Rome!

By the time the cathedral had been completed by another Italian, Santino Solaris, a different archbishop ruled over Salzburg. The proportions laid down in the original plans were reduced, but this was done without diminishing the grandeur and beauty of the building.

In Salzburg large and small things co-exist in perfect harmony: the cathedral is vast; vast, too, is the magnificent fountain in the Residenzplatz. It has three levels, stands 15 meters high, includes some beautiful statues and is generally considered to be one of the greatest baroque fountains in the world. There are other fountains decorated with equestrian motifs, and these are as

Palaces, cultural monuments, fountains, shops and cafés are all an important aspect of Salzburg's character. Even more celebrated is that other aspect of its life: the summer music festival, the performance of "Jedermann" (the famous morality play staged each year in front of the cathedral), the celebrated puppet plays, the concerts in Salzburg's many theaters and the débuts of young and unknown artists anxious to prove their talents.

Who knows if the fair-haired young man with the poetic eyes might not turn out to be a future Mozart?

Everything is possible in Salzburg, where music, sound and *joie de vivre* are the true realities. Here you can forget the violence and fear which, far away from the spot where the waters of the Salzach change their name and their color, torment the hearts of mankind.

VIENNA, LEGEND OF THE PAST, MUSIC OF ETERNITY

Vienna is the pearl of Europe. In Vienna the people are cheerful, steeped in an atmosphere of ancient elegance, surrounded by beautiful monuments, streets and buildings. The air still seems to echo with the music of Strauss and Lehar which accompanies the imperial white horses of the Spanish Riding School, no less famous than the Viennese women.

The Viennese are born with the sound of music in their ears and from their earliest years are given a knowledge of musical instruments. One does not ask a Viennese whether he plays an instrument but which instrument the plays. Vienna boasts one of the best orchestras in the world, the famous Philharmonic, and one of the best opera houses, the Staatsoper, not to speak of a symphony and a chamber orchestra endowed with long traditions.

Walking along the Ring, one of the main avenues of the city and four miles long, we see imposing buildings and wonderful gardens. Along the Ring are the Staatsoper, the Burgtheater, the university, the Naturhistorisches Museum, the Kunsthistorisches Museum (a picture gallery famous all over the world), the parliament building, the Town Hall. In the historic heart of the city one can admire the Gothic cathedral of St. Stephen, whose tower, the highest in the city, is the symbol of Vienna. The Karlskirche, the work of the architect J.B. Fischer, is the most important example of Viennese Baroque, whilst the Votivkirche, whose style imitates the Gothic, is extremely interesting for its sheer architectural imagination.

Every street, every building recalls famous people of the past: the fabulous Schönbrunn, the famous palace of the Habsburgs, the Hofburg and the Belvedere with their memories of Franz Josef and Maria Theresia. In the ancient center of Vienna, in a house in the Schulerstrasse behind the cathedral Mozart composed his finest works, though the house in which he died has now been demolished. A modest but graceful little house in

the Nussdorferstrasse recalls another famous composer, Schubert. This great artist had to wander from place to place seeking the hospitality of friends and relatives (he moved 37 times) while trying to write his best music, including his lieder, sometimes from his hospital bed. It is just as difficult to follow the tracks of Beethoven. This great master was a natural wanderer and moved house 31 times, possibly choosing only lodgings which had a fine view: the most famous was that

of the green hills of the Wiener Wald, where he composed *Fidelio*.

Other places tell of famous men. Sigmund Freud's house near the university is nowadays a museum dedicated to the man and his work.

Vienna: left and above, two of the houses which Beethoven lived in; below, from left to right, two views of Schubert's house and Siegmund Freud's library.

AN ARCHER FOR FREEDOM

Not even the Swiss would claim that Wilhelm Tell actually existed. All the same they have erected a monument in his honor because he is the symbol of their liberty and the architect of the solemn pact of alliance which is seen as the keystone of the Swiss Confederation.

It was in a little meadow on the Rütli or Grütli on the southern shore of Lake Lucerne on 1st August 1291 that a meeting of delegates representing the cantons Unterwalden, Schwyz and Uri was brought together by Wilhelm Tell so that they could take a solemn oath. They swore to support each other for ever through thick and thin, to fight with their wits, money and arms against oppression and injustice, to be ready to do their duty and safeguard their rights and to shake the Swiss nation out of the apathy into which it had fallen.

Switzerland's struggle to free itself from Austrian domination was neither short nor easy, but in 1386 their victory at Sempach finally brought them independence. Later Lucerne was

the only city not to go over to the Protestant faith, instead it kept up the traditions of the Catholic cantons. It became famous for its men of letters and philosophers such as Byron, Shelley and Rousseau and as a result of Friedrich Schiller's *Wilhelm Tell,* published in 1804. Flocks of tourists came from all over Europe to see the birthplace of the legendary archer and hero.

Strangers are made to feel at home in Lucerne. The inhabitants are cordial and open by nature, inclined to joviality and joie de vivre and offering accommodation which is always comfortable even when modest. Lucerne's most famous hotel, the "Grand Hotel National", where César Ritz was once manager and Auguste Escoffier chef, has added as much to the city's fame as Wilhelm Tell. The names of these two men have become symbols of excellence in the hotel indus-

Two views of the Grütli Meadow, on the shores of the Vierwaldstättersee, where the first three Swiss cantons swore mutual allegiance in 1291. Right, the wooden bridge known as the Kapell-brücke at Lucerne, and its famous paintings.

try and haute cuisine.

Lucerne should be visited on foot, crossing its two famous bridges, the Kappellbrücke and the Spreuerbrücke, which span the river Reuss. These are interesting covered bridges decorated with unusual paintings and to some extent are symbols of the city. The Spreuerbrücke dates from the Middle Ages and was rebuilt in the 16th century.

Like all tourists we can stand in front of the "Lions of Lucerne", a monument commemorating the Swiss guards who were killed in the Tuileries during the French Revolution, admire the Glacier Gardens, say a prayer in the Baroque churches, cross the waters of the lake on the steamer, look at the twenty-million-year-old fossil palm fronds in the Ice Age Museum and visit the Transport Museum.

We can return through the streets and squares to wander at leisure over the two covered bridges and then stop again at the Rütli meadow. It would be pleasant to imagine the thirteenth-century archer, surrounded by an anxious and sympathetic crowd, staring at the apple on his son's head and ready, if his hand should falter, to draw another arrow from his quiver to kill the notorious tyrant Gessler, by whose order the apple had been placed there.

But his arrow did not kill the boy, and good triumphed in the end.

MARVELS OF OLD SWITZERLAND

In 882 the monk Meinrad was granted permission by his abbot to take up the life of a hermit, giving himself wholly over to prayer, in the woods of the Finsterwald not far from the lake of Zurich. So it was that he withdrew from the world, dressed in his coarse homespun, with but a crucifix, a small Madonna, and some of his own manuscripts as his total earthly possessions. Not much time passed, however, before the valley people chanced upon his retreat and began coming to him for advice, deeming the holy man to be of worthy counsel. Earnestly concerned to keep his vow, Meinrad pushed on further into the forest, settling in a clearing where two crows were all the company he had. This was where, thirty years later, two ruffians assassinated him. Legend has is that the two crows pursued the murderers and thereby brought about their arrest. In any event, when Brother Nennone came to found the Benedictine Abbey of Ensiedeln in 906 near the ill-fated hermitage, he had Meinrad's faithful companions immortalized as part of the monastery's coat of arms.

Centuries went by. The Benedictine's outreach was to extend further and further beyond Ensiedeln. Emperors and princes were to lavish gifts upon them as a token of appreciation of those works accomplished through *Notre Dame's* intercession. Later, Meinrad was to be canonized and a painting on wood of the "black" (i.e. Benedictine) Virgin was to replace the miraculous Madonna. Reconstructed by Moosbruger at the dawn of the 18th century on the original foundations, the abbey became one of the greatest monasteries of its age. The porticoes, the cloisters with their abundance of stucco and marble, the frescoed walls all make it a masterpiece of Swiss Baroque art. The story of Meinrad's life, some 1,300 early printed works − (some dating from the first half of the tenth century)−and an equal number of old manuscripts, make up the monastery library's priceless collection, a treasure that includes treatises on physics, medicine, zoology that are of unique historic import.

Another abbey that houses still other precious collections is to be found in St. Gallen, a small town in central Switzerland otherwise famed for its lace and embroidery work.

The convent of Einsiedeln and the church of Saint-Gall: splendid specimens of the rococo style.

KOTOR AND
THE MOUTHS OF CATTARO

Kotor or Cattaro is a town on the coast of Yugoslavia at the foot of Mount Lovcen. It was built in the seventh century of the site of the Roman settlement of Acrivium, and like all places which have a long history, changed its name and its political overlord many times, the more so because it forms a magnificent natural harbor and was therefore a tempting prize. In the rear it is protected by the mountains of Montenegro and on the seaward side by the winding and branching narrows which widen out into basins. Similar to fjords, they are known as the Bocche di Cattaro or "Mouths of Kotor".

In 840 there were dangerous attacks by foreign invaders, but from the tenth to the twelfth century Cattaro developed a thriving maritime trade. Initially it was governed by a Byzantine official, then by an official of the Archbishop of Bari, who built several Benedictine monasteries there.

Kotor is a town of great character. Its Venetian walls that marks its boundaries between the riverside, the shore and Mount Lovcen demonstrate its importance in Venetian days. Its narrow streets lead to the Parade Ground and the Clock Tower. The Catholic Cathedral of St. Trifone was built on an ancient Roman site, destroyed by an earthquake in 1563 and rebuilt with the addition of two Baroque belfries. The Orthodox Cathedral of St. Nicholas was erected in 1909.

Like other places in this locality, Kotor resembles the parts of Italy on the other side of the Adriatic in having scenery which is reminiscent of lakes rather than the seaside. In 1380 when Vittor Pisani defeated the Genoese and brought them as prisoners of war to Chioggia, in his mind's eye he saw Cattaro, which had fallen to him two years earlier. The places were much alike, with all the attraction of calm waters and rosy mountains. Kotor: birthplace of men who made a great contribution to Italian culture, men like Spiridone Sirovich, who left this peaceful and beautiful town to go to far off Italy, put on the red shirt of the *Garibaldini* and fight for justice and liberty.

Two views of the Bay of Kotor, in Yugoslavia: which is among the most spectacular scenery in Europe.

VIOLENCE AND SPLENDOR UNDER THE GOLDEN DOME

In 1156, on a wooded hill near to where the river Moskva flows into the Neglinnaya, Yuri Dolgoruki built a primitive wooden *kreml,* a modest citadel which was destroyed several times by fire and besieging Tartars. Nobody could have imagined that this obscure *kreml* in then obscure Moscow would one day become the heart of Russia.

In the course of the centuries the Kremlin did in fact become a formidable citadel with stout bastions almost 20 feet thick and nineteen towers. Within these walls arose palaces, cathedrals, monasteries, theaters museums built by czars great or cruel, by ambitious princes and enlightened but despotic empresses, heroes, saints, usurpers, warriors and great artists. At the end of the fifteenth century Ivan the Great, disappointed by Russain architects, commissioned the Italian Aristotile Fieravanti, by reputation a magician endowed with extraordinary powers, to build a new cathedral in Moscow. Fieravanti built a group of buildings which achieves a happy synthesis of classical Russian and western architectural forms.

To list the wonders of the Kremlin is indeed a formidable task. The oldest and finest of its towers, known as the Tower of the Savior, boasts bells and a complicated clockwork mechanism to ring them. The Corner Arsenal Tower, the Tower of the Trinity, the Tower of the forest, the Water Tower, the Tower of the Czar, the Stone Tower and the Nameless Towers are all different in height and structure and served different purposes.

The Cathedral of the Assumption, with its splendid interior and wealth of holy relics, has five domes and is considered to be the Reims of Russia. Here the metropolitans and patriarchs of the Russian Othodox Church were crowned by the Czar, here they were buried. Of equal interest are the Cathedral of the Annunciation, the floor of which is covered with polished tiles of agate jasper, and the Cathedral of St. Michael.

The Palace of Facets was built at the end of the fifteenth century by Mario Ruffo and Pietro Solario. The enormous Golden Hall (7,000 square feet in area) has a single gilded central pillar.

In the Grand Kremlin Palace, as in the Terem Palace and the Council of Ministers Building, each dynasty has left its mark and shown its desire to outdo the West, whilst at the same time conceding inferiority.

In the Grand Kremlin Palace one must visit the Armory, now a museum, the Ivan the Great Bell Tower, 290 feet high and containing 33 bells covered in bas-reliefs, the Czar's Cannon and the Czar's Bell.

The Kremlin dominates Red Square, which has witnessed all the most important events in Russian history. Outside its walls, near the Gate of the Savior, you can see the Cathedral of St. Basil, covered in different colored domes and the most typically Russian church in the whole country. Built in 1553 over the tomb of the saint, it is surrounded by auxiliary churches, eight which commemorate Ivan the Terrible's victories over the Tartars.

Not far away is the plain red-marble crypt which contains Lenin's tomb. The two buildings, symbols of contrasting ideologies, remind us that despite struggle and conquest there is still the universal hope of security for the present and better times for the future.

The Great Palace and Cathedral of the Kremlin, Moscow: the heart of the eternal Russia.

THREE STREETS
AND A LOVE STORY

The Via Cappello, the Via delle Arche Scaligere, the Via del Pontiere: these are three streets in Verona in which the saddest and most romantic love story took place. Here, accoding to art and legend, Juliet Capulet (Giulietta Capuleti) and Romeo Montague (Romeo Montecchi), two young lovers, were condemned to death by the long-standing feud between their two families.

Romeo and Juliet means, of course, Shakespeare, tho it is true that others before him had hinted at the tragic events of this love story. In the sixth canto of his "Purgatory" Dante Alighieri mentions the two families, the Ghibelline Capulets and the Guelf Montagues, as two families who carried on a destructive vendetta against each other.

According to some critics Shakespeare is able to move us so deeply with his vivid interpretation of the story because he was very young himself when he wrote this, his first tragedy. Juliet was not yet fourteen, Romeo only just seventeen, so the young Shakespeare could all the better understand and express the anxiety, impetuousness, passion and indeed mistakes of youth. The way they react to parents and friends is not based on so-called "real life" but on the way their emotions and minds work. They do not know the reasons for the quarrels and conflicts, they are only aware that they want to love each other.

So like Shakespeare we begin our sentimental journey around Verona. In the Via delle Arche Scaligere is the beautiful, battlemented mediaeval house dating from the days of the Montecchi. Because of the terrible condition of the house we can only admire it from the outside, imagining Romeo leaving it secretly to stand under the balcony of his beloved.

And to see the famous balcony we go to the Via Cappello near the Piazza delle Erbe: this house dates from the thirteenth century, the period of the Capuleti. Recently restored, the balcony overlooks an internal courtyard, and to join Juliet Romeo had to climb over the outside wall.

"O Romeo, Romeo, wherefore art thou Romeo? Call me but love and I'll be new baptized," we reply for Romeo, and there on the wall is an inscription giving in Italian and English the famous lines of the love-scene.

Still seeking to pay tribute to the star-crossed lovers, we go finally to the Via Pontiere,

where there is a former Capuchin convent much admired for its Baroque chapel and its cloisters. In the crypt is an empty tomb—Juliet's.

Empty? Not at all, it is always full of notes, cards, messages of every kind, the naive, pathetic, happy or sometimes desperate testimony of unknown lovers who are reliving the vicissitudes of the love of Romeo and Juliet.

Verona and the old bridge—the setting for the most symbolic of all love stories. The courtyard of the house and the balcony where Juliet waited for Romeo.

JEWELS OF LAKE MAGGIORE

Although it lies between the Alps of Piedmont and Lombardy, which are covered in snow quite early during the winter, Lake Maggiore nonetheless provides those living around it with the benefits of a microclimate. Rose laurels planted in the ground, palmtrees and giant cacti all heighten the amazement of travelers arriving in winter from the Gothard or the Simplon, or even from Milan, the neighboring metropolis, to the point where they are no longer sure of the season. The deep waters of the Verbano (its other name) extend the full lenght of a huge 40-mile basin, resembling the broadening estuary of a river, from Locarno in the north, in the Swiss canton of Ticino, as far as Arona, in Italy. Stresa is situated about half-way along its west bank.

This region, which one occasionally hears about in connection with international terrorist bands, can boast a number of outstanding cultural events, such as the Locarno Film Festival 'or the Musical Weeks at Stresa. It also has a rich and often turbulent history, involving the internecine strife which devastated the neighboring Italian republics and principalities, beginning with the famous war of the Guelfs and the Ghibellines, in which Dante was an unfortunate hero. But the beauty and the changing colors of the lake and the surrounding hills quickly dispel from one's mind these tragic pages of local history, as one lands on one of the Borromean Islands, those lush gems set in the green showcase of the Glauco Verbano, which was celebrated by the 19th-century poet Felice Cavalotti, a clever politician who had chosen this as his final resting-place.

Opposite the Gulf of Pallanza, between Stresa and Punta San Remigio, the Borromean Islands provide a visual treat, with their lavish palaces and the flora of their gardens, some of

which are laid out with full French symmetry while others show the influence of the exuberant romantic English garden; yet others are designed to meet the daily needs of the island-dwellers, as they have done for centuries past.

Both in character and history, each of the four islands is quite distinctive.

The descendants of a certain Vitiliano, prince and soldier, the Borromeo family, which gave the small archipelago its name, reigned over the entire region from the first half of the 15th century onwards. Its was they who developed Isola Madre, named in honor of the Virgin, the patron of a long-lost church, by planting many species of flowers and fruit trees around their sumptuous mansion. It was there that Duchess Cesi, the widow of Cesar Borromeo, who had been killed in action, retired for much of her life to lament her sad loss.

The gardens of Isola Bella, which include large numbers of exotic plants and are laid out over vast terraces, are even more extraordinary. Grottoes, fountains, obelisks, statues, as well as baroque monuments and palaces bear witness to the imagination of the most famous architects and the finest landscape artists of the period. In the midst of this miniature paradise, set apart from the passage of time, who could possibly imagine the rough and barren island which once stood on this site? It is no wonder that so many eminent persons, including Napoleon, chose to stay there over the ages.

San Giovanni and Isola dei Pescatori, on the other hand, did not enjoy the lavish favors of the Borromeos. All that the visitor sees on one of them is a shady wood and the ruins of a small oratory. The other is home to the lake fishermen who keep alive an ancient tradition and whose boats—their sole wealth—still retain their characteristic outline. They tirelessly cast their nets in the green waters of the Verbano and spend a very long day at work, before returning to their cottages, whose lively colors contrast with the dark foliage all around. In spring the open-air cafes *(grotti)* open to coincide with the arrival of the first tourists from northern Europe, come to forget in a few hours the hardships of a long winter.

The enchantment of Lake Maggiore lasts well into autumn: in the little harbor of Brissago, in the Ticino, it is possible to see, late in October, the strange scarlet fruit of an imposing tomato tree transplanted from Patagonia; and throughout the lake area one can often have one's lunch on the balcony on New Year's Day.

Isola Bella (Borromean Islands). In this enchanting setting, on the shores of Lake Maggiore, one can escape to a world of unreal beauty.

LA SCALA, MILAN

The most famous things in Milan are the Madonnina (the tallest spire of the cathedral), la Scala and *pannetone* (a local sweet cake), things of which the Milanese are justly proud because they symbolise faith, art and good food.

Let us leave out the Madonnina, leave to the reader the pleasure of discovering *pannetone,* especially at Christmas, and stop briefly at the opera house which has always been the Mecca of opera-singers.

At the end of the sixteenth century Milan already had an opera house. It was destroyed by fire in 1695, rebuilt in 1699 and burnt down yet again in 1708.

Fire seemed greatly attracted to Milanese theaters, for on 25th February 1776 the new Ducal Theater was burned to the ground by "a Vesuvius which hurled flames and cinders a great distance" according to Pietro Verri, writing to his brother Alessandro. Thus Milan was deprived once again of its principal opera house, but the Milanese, practical-minded as well as fanatical music-lovers, discussed the construction of a new opera house on the site of the church of Santa Maria della Scala.

Once Archduke Ferdinand had given his consent, the commission was given to the architect Piermarini, who had built the marvellous Villa Reale at Monza, considered the Schönbrunn of Italy.

On 3rd August 1778 La Scala opened with a performance of *L'Europa Riconosciuta* by Antonio Salieri, a memorable event and the first of many.

In 1978 La Scala celebrated its bicentenary, and as part of the celebrations a magnificent exhibition traveled all over the world.

In the course of those two centuries Piermarini's great auditorium has seen the rise and fall of operatic idols, has given its seal of approval to young hopefuls such as Bellini, Rossini, Verdi; has mistakenly booed works which later became famous, such as Puccini's "Madame Butterfly"; has been host to composers, conductors, singers, producers, Italian and foreign soloists and spectators obscure or famous, like Stendhal, the "Milanese" as he liked to call himself. Partly destroyed by German bombs, it rose again to continue its noble work. To mention all the names associated

with it would be wrong to many who, for lack of space, one would have to leave out. We think of the costumiers, scene-painters, tailors, dressers and attendants, all the hundreds of people who do their work out of the public eye in the wings and workrooms, the people whom we should thank when the curtain falls and we leave the opera house.

Milan. Left, one of the most famous opera houses in the world: La Scala. Above and right, the famous Victor-Emmanuel Galleries and the central cupola.

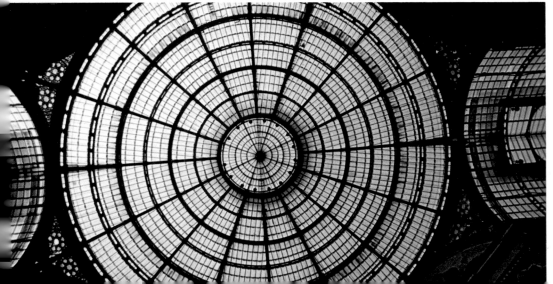

And there is something else which should be mentioned because it is connected with La Scala, the Vittorio Emanuele II Gallery, built by Giuseppe Mengoni and opened on 15th September 1867.

For many years this has served as a sort of foyer or anteroom for La Scala. Here one could feel the pulse of the operatic world and meet all the cultural élite of the city. As Beonio-Brocchieri writes in *I cento anni della Galleria* (Ricordi), after a première "victors and vanquished, traitors and thieves meet in the Gallery in Milan and sip their coffee, as if nothing had happened. What went badly yesterday because of the dread hand of fate will go better tomorrow. There will be advances of salary, engagements: hopes of fame revive."

THE GRAND CANAL, THE MOST UNUSUAL STREET IN THE WORLD

It is said that Amsterdam is the Venice of the North and that Srinagar on Lake Dal is the Venice of India. In reality there is only one Venice; it was founded about 451 A.D. on little islands in the lagoon of the Rivo Alto on the Adriatic by people of the Venetii tribe fleeing from the barbarians.

Since those distant times, many centuries have elapsed and the modest houses built on larch piles have been transformed into splendid palaces, imposing churches in the Gothic Renaissance and Baroque styles and into monasteries. Between one island and the next there is always a bridge (there are more than 400 of them, large and small) so that people can walk the length of Venice, and reach every quarter, square, quayside and canal. And just as every town or country has its main road, Venice's is the Grand Canal or the "Canalazzo" as it is called by the Venetians. This unique highway divides the city into almost equal parts; almost four kilometers in length and in places almost 200 feet wide, dozens of canals flow into it. Every day it is used by craft of all kinds: vaporetti and romantic gondolas, huge barges loaded with goods of all kind, and fast motor-boats which stir up the slow waters of the Grand Canal. Many of the most beautiful and famous buildings in Venice lie along the Grand Canal, palaces best known by the simple name of "Ca'", short for "casa" or house. The wonderful Palazzo Corner, the Ca'Grande, built by Sansovino in 1532, the Ca'Rezzonico, the Ca'Foscari which bears the

same name as the famous Doge, the Palazzo Spinelli and the renaissance Palazzo Tiepolo; the magnificent Grimani built by Sammichele towards the end of the 16th century and the famous Ca'Doro (mistakenly called d'oro) in the Gothic style, the Palazzo Franchetti and the Palazzo Vendramin-Calergi, one of the most exquisite buildings in Venice and the place where Richard Wagner died.

Of course Wagner was not the only great artist to visit the Grand Canal; painters, writers, musicians and poets of all nations have fallen under the spell of the city of a thousand enchantments and admired from every angle the Church of the Salute built by Longhena in 1631, the Riva degli Schiavoni, the Fondaco dei Turchi and the Bridge of Sighs. And like all the tourists they will have crossed the Rialto Bridge which traces its history back to the bridge of boats which first linked its banks in the year 1180.

Having been burnt down several times, and each time rebuilt in wood, it collapsed in 1450 and was at long last replaced in 1592 by a stone structure which the Senate commissioned the providentially named Antonio da Ponte to design. Its arch, which is 72 feet wide and 23 high, was intended to allow war galleys to pass beneath. Nowadays it adds to the heavy but wholly peaceful traffic on the Grand Canal the attractive spectacle of its picturesque shops, which lie at the heart of a perpetually lively commercial district. Unlike Venetians, from whom they can thus be readily distinguished, visitors to Venice always take a long time to cross the Rialto—their minds evidently reeling from the sheer beauty of the

Grand Canal, the palaces and the bridge itself.

And the charming little shops, selling exquisitely made traditional handicrafts such as lace and Murano glass, make this remarkable bridge one of the places in Venice which the visitor should not miss, under any circumstances—one more picture for the camera without which few people pass along the Grand Canal, the most unusual highway in the world.

The Grand Canal, Venice, where it meets the lagoon, and a commemorative celebration. On the right of the photograph above, note the Rialto. Below, the famous Ca d'Oro, model of a Venetian palace of the 15th-century.

THE CITY OF THE SIGNORIA

The traveller to Florence carries in his mind the picture of a city of sweetly-smiling hills, the Arno reflecting the graceful bridges and old houses along its sinuous course, the flower-filled gardens and the beauty of Florentine women. But apart from its wealth of works of art, Florence has another aspect, that of the august and forbidding places whose stone defies time and documents history.

Typical by reason of its majestic bulk is the Palazzo Vecchio, a colossal work of art, which sems to watch over the old heart of ancient Florence from its site in the spacious Piazza della Signoria.

The "Grand Old Man" as it is called with pride and familiarity by the Florentines, was planned and built by the architect Arnolfo di Cambio in 1299.

The city, after a century of faction-fighting between Guelf and Ghibellines, between White and Black (of which even the greatest Italian poet, Dante Alighieri, was a victim), succeeding in settling its differences, installed a government with popular support and subjugated the neighboring cities. The massive crenellated building that dominates Florence, looking more like a fortified castle than a palace, was built to provide a worthy seat for its rulers.

The interior of the Palazzo Vecchio, completely altered in the 1500s, is rich in major works of art: the porphyry fountains designed by Vasari, the famous 16th-century chamber in which the Grand Council used to meet, the 13th-century chamber, rich in frescoes, the apartments of Leo X, Cosimo I and Cosimo "il Vecchio", of Lorenzo il Magnifico and Giovanni of the Black Bands; the Chapel of the Priors, the little office of Francesco I, masterpiece of the Italian Florentine style, the chapel of Eleonora of Toledo with frescoes by Bronzino.

No less magnificent is the Piazza della Signoria where many different styles come together to form a harmonious whole: the Loggia of the Lances, designed by Orcagna about the middle of the 14th century and built to allow the Priors to summon the citizens, is also full of works of art. The most famous is certainly *Perseus* in bronze standing on a magnificent and historical pedestal, a masterpiece by B. Cellini. The splendid *Rape Of The Sabine Women* is ascribed to Giambologna, whilst the statue of *Judith* is the work of Donatello. Also to be seen are a Greek statue, symbols of the cardinal and theological virtues, two splendid lions and the coats of arms of the Guilds and of the City.

The Piazza della Signoria is always teeming with tourists; they come and go from the Palazzo Vecchio and the Uffizi Gallery; they stop in front of the copy of Michelangelo's *David* (today the original is in the Galleria dell'Accademia), and admire the splendid Neptune fountains, made by B. Ammannati in 1575.

Afterwards, their eyes surfeited with masterpieces, and physically worn out with all the to-ing and fro-ing, they sit down in one of the old and famous cafés in the square and, following the noisy flights of the swallows, they drink their well-deserved aperitif with great satisfaction.

Florence: left, the tower of the Palazzo Vecchio as seen from the Giotto Campanile and a view of the Piazza della Signoria. Right, Michelangelo's David, and, in profile, Perseus, by Benvenuto Cellini.

BY THE LOVELY WATERS OF THE ARNO

If one can believe astrology, Dante Alighieri comes under the sign of Gemini, as he was born between 21st May and 7th June 1265. This sign would have given him many virtues and defects, chiefly ability, impetuosity and a great breadth of interests.

The family of the future poet was descended, it was said, from the Romans who settled Florence, and the founder of the family, Cacciaguida (1110 to circa 1147), took part in the Second Crusade. The Alighieri minor gentry of the Guelf persuasion, without great economic resources but not poor.

There has been a great deal of discussion as to which house Dante was born and lived in. In 1911 the municipality of Florence constructed a medieval building with this inscription: "I was born and grew up in the great city by the lovely waters of the Arno". In these lines from the *Inferno* the poet reveals to two of the Damned that he is a Florentine.

However, the house in which Dante lived was pulled down, as Indro Montanelli points out in *Dante e il suo secolo* (Rizzoli), when he was proscribed in 1302 for political reasons. He and three other Florentines were accused of "having disturbed the peace of Pistoia by persecuting those of the Black Party (Dante was a Guelf and a White), of having opposed the Pope and the house of Valois and of having broken the law by improperly influencing the election of city officials." Although the penalties were severe, the accused did not appear for trial, their cases went by default and they were condemned to death. In accordance with the law, Dante's house was demolished "down to its very foundations". This house was near the former Abbey of Santa Maria. Nowadays, the opening at the corner of the Via Santa Margherita is the site of the *Case delli Alighieri*. Number 1 is the entrance to the Alighieri house and the Dante Museum (apparently his birthplace is number 4 in the street which now bears his name, formerly Via S. Martino). We can imagine Dante as a boy roaming those narrow mediaeval streets around the Torre della Castagna, once the headquarters of the Priori dei Arti before the Palazzo Vecchio was built.

Baptized in the church of S. Giovanni, he spent his early years in a brick-built house with wooden shutters at its unglazed windows. On cold days the fire-places were hardly able to take the chill off the air, and cloaks and hats were worn even indoors. But Dante was unlikely to have spent much time at home. He exactly reflected the Florence of his day, passionate and talented, fiery, a harbinger of the Renaissance, he loved his studies as much as he loved the pleasures of life. In his disordered and wandering life, characterised by furious outbursts of anger and impulsive generosity, there was one fixed and constant star: Beatrice. When he saw her for the first time at a feast, she was dressed in red and just nine years old, whilst he was ten. He saw her again nine years later in her white wedding dress, and six years afterwards she died. When he had come through a serious crisis of religious belief, Dante applied himself even more diligently to his studies, philosophy and the quest for truth and justice. This involved him in political activity, and in due course changes in political fortunes led to his exile. In 1295 he entered into a loveless marriage with Gemma Donati, who gave him two children. He sought refuge all over Italy, coming to Ravenna in 1313, where he died in 1321.

In the palace belonging to Guido da Pollenta, his generous host, he finished the 15,000 lines of his *Divina Commedia,* longing all the time

MCMXI
TRA LA CHIESA DI SAN MARTINO DEL VESCOVO
E LE ABITAZIONI DEI DONATI E DEI MARDOLI
SORGEVANO CONTIGUE LE CASE
DI BELLO E BELLINCIONE ALIGHIERI
E NELL'AVITA DIMORA NACQVE DANTE

IL COMVNE DI FIRENZE
SI ASSICVRÒ IL POSSESSO DEL LVOGO
E SVLLE VESTIGIA DELLE ANTICHE CASE
COSTRVI QVESTO EDIFICIO
PER NVOVA PVBBLICA ONORANZA
AL DIVINO POETA

He was a painter, sculptor, architect, mathematician, scientist, anatomist, alchemist and botanist. The multiplicity of his interests was such that he often stopped working on a commission he had already started, making an important patron wait a long time for his work, so that he could devote himself to research which is still of interest today.

His paintings are few in number, but include the *Mona Lisa, Leda,* the *Annunciation,* the *Virgin of the Rocks, St. Sebastian,* and *La Belle Ferronnière.* Some of them, such as the *Last Supper* in Santa Maria delle Grazie in Milan, are in a poor state of preservation because da Vinci was experimenting with a new technique of fresco painting in order to achieve a new chromatic mixture. The experiment turned out to be disastrous for the future state of this marvellous painting, and damp also played its part.

Leonardo lived in Florence, Venice, Mantua, and Rome, favored by princes and rich art-lovers. Amongst those of his inventions which have survived are the "fabulous devices" invented for entertainments, great weddings and festivities. Amongst so many one can mention merely the *paradiso* made for the wedding of Isabella of Aragon and Duke Gian Galeazzo Visconti and the lion constructed for François I. This had an internal mechanism which enabled it to walk the length of a room, whereupon its chest opened to display the *fleur de lys* of France. France was to be the country in which he would find his last resting-place, after having served two of her kings. Amongst his pupils was Luini, the grace of whose canvases reminds us of Leonardo himself, Sodoma, who had such an important influence on the Sienese School, and his favorite Francesco de' Melzi, his artistic heir, but surrounded as he was by talented youths, eminent men and famous beauties, he chose solitude as his ideal, saying "Be alone and you will be truly yourself".

An inscription in the chapel of the château of Amboise tells us that beneath it rest the bones found when the old chapel was excavated. Amongst them are thought to be the mortal remains of Leonardo da Vinci.

BIRTHPLACE OF A LEGENDARY MAN

From time to time destiny brings great fame to a very unimportant place. That is exactly what has happened to Vinci, between Empoli and Florence, where Leonardo was born in a farm house.

Vinci was only a group of houses by a hill crowned by a castle, and the notary Master Piero would never have dreamt for one moment that the baby born in 1452 from his liason with a certain Caterina would bring glory and fame to Vinci. Master Piero would have liked the boy to follow him in the law, but quite early in Leonardo's life Piero realised how different the boy's interests were. It is known that in 1467 Leonardo went to Florence to work in the studio of Andrea Verrocchio alongside Botticelli and Perigino.

Leonardo had a universal view of life. For him the physical and psychological aspects of man were of equal importance. He investigated everything, the structure of an animal or a leaf, with a critical eye. For him it was not enough to transfer a figure to canvas with his brushstrokes, he had to show the texture of a cloth, the curve of a curl, the delicacy of a hand at rest, in such a way as to express the subject's innermost feelings in every detail. Acute curiosity and sensitivity are Leonardo's essential characteristics.

Left, ornamental motifs from the façade of the Palazzo Vecchio; Dante's house, with commemorative plaque. Right and below, the birthplace of the greatest genius of all, Leonardo da Vinci (reproduction).

ON THE COLLE DEL PARADISO

The Colle del Paradiso, or Hill of Paradise, on the low southern slopes of Mount Subiaco in Umbria, is the site of the basilica dedicated to St. Francis of Assisi. To all intents and purposes Assisi began its existence in 1181 on the very day St. Francis was born there, the man the world would call *il Serafico* (the Seraphic One) and *il Poverello* (the Poor Little One). Nobody now gives any thought to the fact that the town was founded by the Etruscans and then shared the fate of the other Tuscan towns, falling in turn under Roman, Barbarian, Byzantine and finally ecclesiastical domination. If we talk of Assisi or visit Assisi, it is because it is a place which retains an almost unreal atmosphere of sweetness and love, as if time had come to a stop within its walls.

Before climbing the hill, let us go to Santa Maria degli Angeli, the great basilica containing the Porziuncola, the rough, time-blackened chapel where St. Francis used to pray and where he gathered together his first brethren.

They say that in Assisi everything is for looking at rather than talking about. The Romanesque cathedral dedicated to St. Rufino was rebuilt in 1217 to the designs of Giovanni da Gubbio and has a wonderful façade. Here the Emperor Frederick II and St. Francis were baptized. The Bell Tower dates from the ninth century.

The Basilica of St. Francis and the Holy Convent are the most famous ecclesiastical buildings. The basilica consists of two churches: the mediaeval Lower Church with the high altar over the tomb of St. Francis and the light-filled Upper Church in French Gothic style, rich in

works of art including frescoes by Giotto, Cimabue, Lorenzetti, Martini, etc.

The Temple of Minerva was described by Goethe as a gem, the Torre Communale of 1200 is solid and charming at the same time, and the Piazza Maggiore is a happy blend of Ancient Rome, the Middle Ages and the Renaissance. Other delights are the porch of the Chapel of St. Bernardino, the Cathedral of Santa Chiara, the Hermitage of the Carceri and the richly-stocked Library.

The "official" information on Assisi is given in all the tourist guidebooks, but the latter are unsatisfying, perhaps unnecessary. Whether you are a believer or an atheist, once you enter the walls of Assisi you will be enthralled by the air you breathe there. You almost expect to come across the Pietro Bernardino who locked his rebellious adolescent son under the stairs, that son as yet untouched by God's grace. You will think of beautiful Chiara ("Clare") degli Scifi, for whom the saint founded the Order of Poor Clares and see her in the garden of the Convent of St. Damian, where St. Francis, near his end in May 1226, wrote his Song of Creation, his sublime spiritual testament. You will be fascinated by the chapels, stained-glass windows, frescoes, rose-windows, relics, little streets, the landscape and the very color of the walls. And it will not surprise you that in 1230, whilst the saint's remains were being transferred in solemn procession from the little church of St. George to the nearly-finished basilica, a group of armed men ran in, stole the coffin, rushed off to the cathedral and closed up its walls. For centuries nobody knew why this had happened, nor where the coffin was now hidden. However, in 1818 the tomb was found in the rock under the high altar.

In the beautiful heartland of Umbria: Assisi, where St. Francis lived and worked. Left, general view, the saint's birthplace and the old basilica. Below, the interior of the new basilica (13th-century).

THE APPIAN WAY, REGINA VIARUM

The Roman Censor Appius Claudius was blind but his mind was very acute. He realized that goods, travellers, carts and, most important of all, the army that was to defend Rome from possible attack could move more quickly over paved roads than over unpaved tracks. His idea was accepted and in 312 BC work started on what would become the most important Roman road.

Appius Claudius personally supervised the workmen and stone-masons and with his own bare feet tested the levelness of the blocks of basalt, a volcanic rock of great hardness. These blocks were arranged in the manner of a mosaic and fitted together so perfectly that neither traffic nor the passage of the centuries have been able to dislodge them. Today the Appian Way has been asphalted over, but where the ancient paving comes to the surface it is possible to see the care with which the road was constructed more than two thousand years ago.

The Romans, justly proud of their achievement, called this road *Regina Viarum,* the Queen of Roads. Starting from the Porta Capena, it ran to the rival city of Capua and was then extended as far as Brindisi; several centuries later the great Emperor Trajan built a branch road which reached Brindisi by an easier route. This stretch was known as the Via Appia Trajana. The original Via Appia Antica is extremely impressive. It passes temples and villas such as the one in which Seneca, the great philosopher, opened his veins at Nero's orders and awaited death in earnest discussion with his disciples. Tombs and monuments recall Romans both famous and unknown such as the graves of the Horatii and Curiatii and the famous tomb of Cecilia Metella.

The Appian Way is more than 700 km long and is full of associations with historical figures first encountered in school-books: Pompey the Great, Julius Caesar who exclaimed "Alea jacta est!" on crossing the Rubicon, Nero, Cicero (buried near Formia) and Spartacus who organised the slave revolt which was put down with great slaughter by the Romans, who crucified six thousand rebels along the Appian Way.

At times the difficulties of paving the *Regina Viarum* were enormous because of marshes, broken ground and masses of rock which had to be levelled. Nowadays drivers passing along this stretch of the Appian Way, known locally as "the ribbon of Terracina", near the town of the same name about 100 km from Naples, do not realise the sophisticated level of engineering skills needed to build this amazing project.

Rome, the Via Appia which was opened in 312 AD; its monuments and tombs are perhaps the most moving of all those produced by ancient Rome.

THE FORUM ROMANUM

Tarquinius Priscus, last king of Rome but one, built the Cloaca Maxima to drain the low-lying land to the north of the Palatine. Thus the vast marsh where in earlier times Sabines and Romans had met (and where historians say there was a necropolis in even more remote times) now became a great level expanse of ground which was to be the site of the first and most important monument of the Rome of the Caesars, the Forum Romanum.

It was 390 feet long and 260 feet wide and lay between the Capitoline and the Palatine Hills.

Hence it soon became the center of public life, where citizens met to discuss business, politics and any other problem which affected the life of the city. It was surrounded by colonnades, shops and monuments. Many temples stood on the site: the Temple of Vesta built by order of Numa Pompilius, the Temple of Castor and Pollux, the Basilica Julia, the Temple of Saturn and the Aerarium. Opposite the Temple of Vespasian was the Temple of Concord, with its many beautiful columns, and the Tabularium. To the north-east were the Mamertine Prison and the Curia— the setting for the assemblies of the people and public meetings to discuss matters of trade or law. Apart

from the Temple of Jupiter, a most important site was the Imperial Rostra or orator's tribune, from which speeches could be made to the people.

From Republican times in the fifth century B.C. until the fall of the Empire, the Forum, in the splendor of its statues, columns and triumphal arches, mirrored the glory of Rome itself. Despite defeat in battle and the attacks of invaders it still survived until, by a tragic irony, it was the sons of Renaissance Rome who pulled down the remains and used the marbles to rebuild St. John Lateran, thus according the Forum the same fate as the Colosseum. The Forum Romanum remained the *Campo Vaccino* or "Field of Cattle" until in 1800

Pope Pius VII ordered the start of excavations which were to uncover a thousand years of history.

Rome: overall view of the ruins of the Forum; left, the gigantic Colosseum.

UP AND DOWN THE SPANISH STEPS

Sitting on the steps is a sixteen-year-old with short curly hair and dark skin. He is shyly touching the strings of a guitar and quietly humming "Arrivederci Roma". Further away, a fair-haired Scandinavian couple with rucksacks on their backs are staring at a map of Rome and munching apples. Up and down the steps of the Piazza di Spagna flows a varied stream of people of all ages, races and colors with cameras, rucksacks, shoulder-bags, recorders and guitars. Someone is selling prints, someone else dashing off caricatures of interested passers-by, over there a beautiful girl from Trastevere and her boyfriend are plaiting delicate threads of copper and steel and threading brightly-colored beads for necklaces and earrings, which they sell at bargain prices.

Such an amazing variety of people might possibly remind one of a sort of *Cour des miracles,* but in fact the atmosphere is very different from Victor Hugo's, and the faces of the crowd express lively interest and quiet contentment. They really enjoy being here.

Lorenzo Bernini, the most eminent sculptor of the baroque period, designed the *Fontana della Barcaccia.* Rich though his imagination was, he could not have forseen that a few centuries later flocks of foreign tourists would linger beside its famous waters to enjoy the cool air on sultry summer evenings.

Do these foreign tourists sitting on the steps know anything of the history of the fountain, the Obelisk or the church of the Trinità dei Monti?

The church, started in 1495 by order of King Charles VIII of France, was consecrated by Pope Sixtus V in 1585. After the neglect it suffered during the Napoleonic period, the restoration work done by Francesco Mazois was paid for by Louis XVIII, and its *fleurs-de-lys* date from that period.

Nowadays the church is in the care of the Order of the Sacred Heart, and only part of it is open to the public. It has some outstanding works of art, including some by Raphael, Sodoma and Daniele da Volterra, Michelangelo's most outstanding pupil.

On the hilltop of the Trinità dei Monti is the Obelisk of Sallust, which in classical times stood in the Gardens of Sallust near the Porta Salaria. It is covered in ancient Egyptian symbols and hieroglyphics. Pope Pius V had it set up in front of the church in 1789.

Let us stand and look down for a moment, leaning on the balustrade: on the famous flight of steps adorned with the coat of arms of Pius V, two great Corinthian capitals and some Renaissance bas-reliefs some young people are still lingering in conversation and listening to the murmur of the city while they wait for the moon to rise over the Piazza di Spagna and the Via Condotti, one of the most famous streets in the world. It is a sight never to be forgotten.

Rome: the basilica of Trinità-dei-Monti and the spectacular stairs which lead down to the Piazza di Spagna. Below, the famous fountain on that same square.

THE HOUSE OF THE FATHER OF ALL

This was how Pope Pius XII once described St. Peter's, Rome, in the course of a talk he was giving to married couples. St. Peter's is the greatest church in Christendom and those who behold it are always amazed by the perfection of its geometry and the wealth of its art treasures.

The enormous circular colonnade of the Piazza San Pietro, designed by Lorenzo Bernini, seems to throw open its arms in welcome to the world. The best view of the piazza is from the two rounded stones between the fountains on either side of the obelisk. Thanks to the masterly use of perspective the row of columns appears to consist of only one. The columns, 184 of them, stand on 88 pilasters disposed in four orders and are surmounted by 164 statues.

Because St. Peter was martyred and buried on the Vatican, also known as the Circus of Nero, the Emperor Constantine chose it as the site of his original basilica, named after the apostle. In the early sixteenth century Bramante was given the task of demolishing the old building, which was threatening to collapse, and constructing the new basilica, the first stone of which was laid on 18th April 1506. The work lasted for a hundred years, long after the original architect and his

lantern. Inside the church there are two other large domes; 229 columns in marble, 533 in travertine, 16 in bronze; 104 statues in marble, 161 in travertine, 40 in bronze, 90 in plaster; 44 altars and eight lesser domes. The nave is 615 feet long and at its center a huge disk of porphyry marks the spot where the Emperor Charlemagne was crowned in the year 800 A.D.

But these figures leave out of account the infinite beauty of St. Peter's, which cannot be conveyed in a cold, schematic catalog. In this great cathedral you must enter with your eyes ready to take in its riches and enough sensitivity to share the joys and sorrows of the artists who have poured out their faith and their talent over a period of 400 years in the form of canvas, stone, marble, and precious metals. Think for instance of the young Michelangelo carrying out his first major work, the famous Pietà, the only work to bear his signature. Then stop at the chapels, doorways, funerary monuments, paintings the Chapel of the Blessed Sacrament with its impressive tabernacle, St. Peter's Chair, Bernini's masterpiece of the goldsmith's art. To have a really good look at St. Peter's one visit is not enough, however good your concentration. But in the end, with the best will in the world, exhausted by one's wanderings, confused by the names of so many

patron had died. It was carried on by Raphael, Michelangelo, Vignota, Algardi, Giacomo della Porta and Domenico Fontana. In the piazza the latter put up the obelisk brought to Rome by Caligula and then erected in the Circus of Nero. Michelangelo's dome was finished in 1590, and the façade was completed by Carlo Maderno. Finally the new basilica was consecrated by Pope Urban VIII on 18th November 1626.

Those who like figures and statistics will be interested to know that the dome, built in only 22 months, measures 435 feet to the top of the

popes, famous people and artists, one will not be able to remember much. So it is better to return there again and again, to kiss the feet of the bronze statue of St. Peter, to visit the holy grotto, the sacristy and the treasury, to climb to the top of the dome, if you do not suffer from vertigo.

Above and top right: aerial views of the gardens and palace of the Vatican. Right: St. Peter's basilica, with a detail from the ceiling of the central vault.

SEE NAPLES AND...

The old saying goes "see Naples and die", but I hold the view that it would be better to go on living, even if only to have another look at Naples, that city famous for reasons both good and bad, and to surrender to the enchantments of its peerless bay (the witch Circe lived in these parts, didn't she?).

If one looks at the map one sees famous placenames which recall people and events from the distant past, from the Virgilian Campi Flegrei at Caserta to the Islands of Procida, Ischia and Capri and the peninsula of Sorrento, joining Sorrento, Positano, Amalfi and Paestum. Each place has a long and varied history to relate, glorious periods such as that of Amalfi, a city of one of the most powerful maritime republics of the thirteenth century, which, though nowadays it no longer possesses a powerful fleet, still retains an extraordinary grace and fascination. There is Paestum with its lovely Doric temples, and Caserta with its wonderful royal palace built by Vanvitelli and its valuable collections of Capodimonte work... No less interesting are the relics of Roman, Byzantine, Angevin, Norman, Spanish, Bourbon and French rule. Villas, gardens, monasteries (one of the finest in Naples, San Michele, is now a luxury hotel) all feed one's imagination and enable it to wander back through the centuries. Whilst we linger by the Lake of Averno or by the fumaroles of the sulphur mines, we can also recall that we are at the foot of a volcano which woke up in a very bad mood many centuries ago.

Above: on the shores of the Tyrrhenian Sea, the delightful setting of Amalfi and, top right, against the azure sky of Capri, the famous Villa San Michele.

THE LAST DAYS OF POMPEI

On the 24th of August 79 AD, the little town at the foot of Vesuvius, amongst the orange trees and gardens, was sweltering in the heat of the day. Through seven gates and along the Street of Abundance, merchants and travellers streamed to rejoin their families and friends in this little Campania town. It was 17 years since a great earthquake had destroyed most of the place and its reconstruction had not yet been completed. Much had been destroyed, but the theater built in the second century BC and extended under the Emperor Augustus still stood, as did the baths, the oldest and largest of which were the Stabian Baths. And there were the shops and the Forum where the townspeople met to talk politics and business.

But living at the foot of a volcano entails a grave risk: on that ill-fated August 24th, whilst the inhabitants of Pompei were having their midday meal, Vesuvius exploded. Red-hot stones, volcanic ash and rivers of lava poured down the side of the mountain, demolishing walls, carrying everything before it with a destructive fury made more sinister by a thunderstorm. The dragon's breath brought death and destruction to the whole valley.

This terrible disaster was so sudden and so violent that most of the inhabitants of Pompei were killed. It was not until 1748 that excavations unexpectedly brought to light a town of immense archaeological importance. Villas with frescoes of great interest both because of the scenes they depicted and because of their colors, including the famous *"Pompeyan red"*, houses with rooms grouped round an open atrium and a garden at the back onto which the bedrooms opened. The

famous sites are the Villa of the Mysteries with its extensive frescoes, the House of the Surgeon with its surgical instruments, the House of the Faun, the Villa of Boscoreale with its valuable silverware now in the Louvre, and the House of Menander, now in the Museo Nazionale in Naples.

The finds document the daily life of the citizens of Pompei, from the very structure of the city to its shops. The baker's oven is still full of loaves, on another bench eggs are laid out for sale, and in another merchant's booth the coins still lie where they were left. The lava buried everything, but the archeologists have pumped liquid plaster into the cavities left by the bodies of the dead, thus obtaining casts of the inhabitants of Pompei as they fled, giving us authentic and dramatic evidence of their attempts to survive.

In the earthquake of 1980 Pompei once again suffered severe damage, but the work of restoration is in hand and millions of visitors will be able to admire the rare frescoes and mosaics and imagine the merchants selling cloth, wine and seafood, and the landowners and rich patricians enjoying the pleasures of life and forgetting or ignoring how dangerous it is to live at the foot of a volcano.

Pompei: the remains of the streets and, above, the Forum.

MYCENAE RICH IN GOLD

"Mycenae"—the word recalls those story-books in which, once upon a time, one tried to follow the complicated adventures of Homeric heroes.

Agamemnon, Clytemnestra, Aeneas, Menelaus, Priam, the fair Helen... these are legendary beings which have inspired the imagination of poets of every period and led famous archaeologists or enthusiastic amateurs to seek the solution to one of the most fascinating puzzles in history.

The German Heinrich Schliemann, the most famous of these "amateurs", and his young Greek wife, Sophia Ergastromenos, spent their entire fortune on this quest. It did not matter that Heinrich was 47 and Sophia only 19. All their lives they had two things in common, love and a longing to discover whether the events told in Homer's Iliad had really happened.

Mycenae in Argolis was one of the oldest Greek cities in the Peloponnese. After many a battle with the local authorities Schliemann managed to start his excavations there in 1876. They were continued later by the Greek Archaeological Society and then the English School of Archaeology. From the start to the present time they have brought to light treasures of inestimable value and monuments of outstanding interest.

Mycenae has emerged as a center in which the great Mycenaean civilisation grew up, flourished in the second millenium B.C. and was associated with the initial stage of Cretan civilisation. At an altitude of 910 feet above sea level the acropolis stands out with its encircling Cyclopean walls. Through the monumental Gate of the Lions, so called because it is surmounted by two lionesses standing rampant with their paws resting on a column, one enters the royal necropolis.

Here were found the tombs which Schliemann thought were those of the House of Atreus. They were full of furniture and household goods of the sixteenth century B.C.

It is difficult to imagine how intense and overwhelming was the emotion felt by Heinrich and Sophia when, their hands and nails soiled with earth, rumpled and exhausted by their long excavations, they uncovered the damascened weapons and golden masks of the dead and the embossed furniture which had remained buried for centuries.

Many other ruins and tombs were brought to light in the course of time, amongst which were the "Treasury of Atreus", the "Tomb of Clytemnestra" and the "Cistern of the Perseids". But how many mysteries are still hidden under that ground?

Mycenae, the fabled city of Agamemnon; Knossos, the fabled city of Minos, the legendary king, son of Zeus and Europa.

The palace of Knossos on the island of Crete was discovered by the English archaeologist Evans in 1911. It is an enormous structure with bedrooms, frescoed halls, a throne room, courtyards, staircases, in sum, a palace which hummed with the life of the whole city.

In the Labyrinth was imprisoned the Minotaur, the monster born of the white bull of Poseidon and Pasiphaë, wife of Minos. Fed from time to time with young human victims, it was killed by Theseus with the help of Ariadne, daughter of the king.

Left: Mycenae, the Lion Gate, and (this page) remains of the ancient Royal Palace of Knosses: the two cradles of all Western civilization.

DELPHI OF THE ORACLE

The Pythia, priestess of Apollo, used to sit on a tripod covered in snakeskins, python skins to be precise, hence her name. The place chosen by the Greeks was certainly the most suitable one for a sanctuary which gave auspices as to the future of the nation's warriors and other matters of great importance.

At the foot of Mount Parnassus, the mountain sacred to the Muses, who were said to live with Apollo, rise the two great rocks of the Phaedriades. From a deep cleft rises a spring swathed in steam: this became the Sacred Spring. Naturally wrapped in mist, surrounded by magnificent scenery, perched majestically on a high spot, where frequent thunder and the sounds of water coursing down a thousand mountain streams seemed to tell of mysterious subterranean beings: no other spot could have provided a better setting for the oracle. It soon became the most famous and venerated in all Ancient Greece.

Other temples sprang up next to the Sanctuary, amongst which the most interesting was the circular temple of the Marmaria (6th century B.C.) Circular buildings, or *Tholoi*,

though common in the pre-Hellenic era, are rare in classical times. Of the temple of the Marmaria little remains, alas, except for three columns and the circular platform which was its floor, but these are sufficient to show how buildings can give the faithful a sense of strength and grace combined, a harmony which transcended mere forms to become a real spiritual harmony of interior serenity. This is precisely what one asked of the gods.

In the archaeological site at Delphi one can see the town including its necropolis, the Castalian Spring, which still flows as it did many centuries ago, and the temples. The archaeological finds displayed in the Museum show the high standard attained by archaic Greek sculpture. Of these the finest is the pediment of the *Treasury of Siphnos*. "Treasuries" were buildings put up almost always near temples, for the safekeeping of gifts and votive offered to the gods, and were usually decorated like temples. The fragments of the pediment and other parts of the *Treasury of Siphnos* shows the high standard of taste and subtlety reached by the Greek sculptors of the time. The combat of Apollo and Herakles for the possession of the Delphian tripod, the battle between gods and giants, the assembly of the

gods, the foray of the Dioscuri in the *metope* (square spaces richly decorated with reliefs and alternating with the supporting beams resting on the colonnade) are all examples of rare beauty, for they bear the salient characteristic of the full flowering of Ionian art in the sixth century B.C.

The tension of the muscles of both animals and humans, their postures, the richness of the draperies, the smooth flow of the hair, the intense facial expressions, the armor of warriors preparing to strike or to defend themselves, everything speaks in a language which is far from dead, on the contrary it is very modern and makes one long to transpose that lost world into the present day, so that whether in combat, victory or defeat we could always attain that exterior harmony which reflects interior serenity.

Above: the sanctuary of Athena at Delphi, one of the most famous temples in Greece, and the Sacred Way leading to the temple of Hera. Left, the tiered seats in the theater and, right, the ravine in which the Pythia uttered her oracles.

THE TEMPLE OF THE GODDESS

Pericles, the leader of the republican regime in Athens in 444-430 B.C. has passed into history under the name of Olympicus because of his vigorous oratory. And since all the arts flourished under his administration and the finest monuments in the city can be ascribed to his influence, his age was called the Periclean, or better still, the Golden.

Pericles lived for 70 years, from 499 to 429, and during his lifetime he summoned the greatest geniuses of the period to work for Athens. One of these is considered the very symbol of that age: Pheidias, sculptor, engineer, architect and incomparable genius when it came to creating works of total harmony.

The Parthenon, the temple dedicated to Pallas Athena, goddess of wisdom, and built on the summit of the Acropolis by the architects Ictinos and Callicrates under the direction of Pheidias, is universally regarded as a masterpiece of Greek classicism. Its perfection comes from the absolute balance between dimension and form, between perspective techniques resulting from the slight curvature of apparently straight lines and the free-ranging inventiveness which adds a happy touch of innovation to the Doric style.

The temple consists of a quadrilateral with 17 columns along its length and 8 along its width. It measures just under 230 feet by 100 and stands on a triple base. The two pediments, about 60 feet high, were decorated with splendid bas-reliefs which illustrated a number of scenes from the birth and life of Athena, battle scenes, processions in honor of the goddess, one of the greatest of Greek goddesses, wrestling and animal sacrifices. In the middle of the *cella* or sanctuary, closed off by a bronze railing, was the wonderful statue of Athena sculpted by Pheidias.

Like most other monuments of Antiquity, the Parthenon has been subject to the misfortunes caused by time and mankind, becoming in turn a

Byzantine church, a cathedral and (with the addition of a minaret) a mosque. Explosions, sieges and earthquakes have broken some of the columns and damaged the interior as well. Most of the sculptures were removed by archaelogists and are now in the British Museum and in the Museum of the Acropolis in Athens itself, while the Medici Athena can be seen at the Louvre and the Athena Parthenos (Athena the Virgin) at the Museo Nazionale Archeologico in Florence.

The bas-reliefs are extremely interesting for two reasons: first the imagination and harmony of their composition (despite their being the work of different artists) which proves beyond doubt the uniqueness of the mind which guided their creation, and second the way in which they show the faith of the Athenian people in their goddess and their gratitude for her protection in battle and in their daily lives.

The very symbol of civilization: the Acropolis in Athens. Bottom, the Parthenon with a Corinthian capital in the foreground, and a detail of the frieze.

THE TEMPLE OF OLYMPIAN JOVE

In honor of Jove, or more precisely Olympian Zeus, the Dorians built a temple in Elis, and around it a town soon sprang up, taking the name of Olympia. These events took place in the first half of the fifth century B.C., known to scholars as the period of transition between the archaic and classical periods.

The temple built in 456 B.C. was completed with the help of the most eminent architects and artists of the day. The bas-reliefs of the pediments and the metopes were carved out by a sculptor known only as the "Master of Olympia". He spent a year there working in such themes as the labors of Herakles, the chariot race between the Centaurs and Lapiths in the presence of Apollo, in the course of which the legend tells that the Centaurs tried to carry off the women of the Lapiths. Each of these sculptures is created with an extraordinary sense of power and of balance, and using ingenious devices such as arranging the figures at each end on their knees, in a bending position or semi-reclining in order to adapt them perfectly to the triangular shape of the pediment.

In the internal *cella* stood the statue of Zeus, a masterpiece by Pheidias, the greatest sculptor of the age of Pericles and entrusted by the latter with the task of rebuilding the Parthenon in Athens. The gold and ivory statue of the father of the gods was the largest and most beautiful ever seen and effectively discouraged Pheidias, colleagues from attempting to imitate it.

Today Olympia is a wonderful collection of ruins. Its harmoniously fluted columns are almost all lying amongst the grass, and the remains of this place, more than any other, give one a sense of serenity and peace.

The surrounding countryside is pleasant and bucolic, vines alternating with olives and prickly pears on the terraced hillsides. In the green pastures flocks graze peacefully, whilst women spin wool as in the days of Penelope.

Once Olympia was the scene of great games in honor of the gods, occasions which took place every four years. They became so famous that from the year 776 B.C. onwards the Greeks numbered their years according to the Olympiads which began when the great tripod was lit.

In the shrine of Olympian Zeus one little street is even today bordered with inscriptions bearing the name, not of the winner of this or that competition, as you might think, but of a youth who was guilty of misconduct at the games. He was immortalised so that his disgraceful example would warn those who came after him.

Could we not use the same idea today?

Olympia, the setting for the Olympic Games in ancient times. Top: the tunnel through which competitors passed before entering the stadium, and the threshold from which races started. Below: the gymnasium and remains of the temple.

THE CITY OF ARMS
AND MARZIPAN

In a city like Toledo there are many things to note, but the most famous is the *Fábrica de Armas* which produces weapons (mainly swords and the like) of outstanding workmanship. Many of them, signed by the craftsmen and beautifully engraved and worked in gold, can be seen in various museums.

One of the cities of New Castile, Toledo is sited on a granite eminence 458 meters above sea level and is washed on three sides by the Tagus, which is crossed by the Bridge of Alcántara and that of San Martín. Its origins are very ancient, perhaps Greek or Phoenician, and it was conquered by the Romans in 192 B.C., becoming known as Toletum.

As time went by its importance increased, especially in the sixth century A.D., when it was chosen as the residence of the Visigothic kings and the venue for important councils of the church. When the Arabs conquered the city for the Caliph of Córdoba they took away its privileges as a capital city, and there was a serious uprising. In later years its fortunes rose and fell, but in 1085 it was reconquered by Alfonso VI of León and Castile. Two years after this Toledo became the capital of the kingdom of Castile and thus the focal point of the political, cultural, religious and ecclesiastical life of the state.

The rich local Jewish community had made a valuable contribution to the city's increasing commercial prosperity, but nevertheless at the end of the fifteenth century it was expelled, causing a serious decline in Toledo's economy. An even more serious blow fell in 1560, when Philip II decided to transfer his capital to Madrid. The city, whose archbishops had always been an important spiritual and political force, lost its

power and pre-eminence. It was occupied by the French from 1808 to 1813, and during the Civil War (1936-1939) its Alcazar, manned by officer cadets, put up a desperate resistence against the besieging republican forces until it was relieved by the nationalists.

Toledo is one of the most interesting cities in Spain, not only because, being the oldest Spanish archdiocese, its religious life remains very intense, but also because every street-corner, street or quarter leading down to the river tells a story of the conquerors who have left their mark here. This can be seen in the monuments, streets, palaces, the synagog, the many churches. The

cathedral, started in 1200, has a design which resembles that of the French Gothic churches. The church of Santo Cristo de la Luz was used as a mosque under the Arab domination and before that had been a Visigothic church. The church of Santo Tomás has the *Burial of Count Orgaz* by El Greco.

Nowadays Toledo has varied commercial activity: ceramic factories, agricultural products, woolen and silk textiles. But after having admired its art treasures, the monuments of its past and its natural beauties, allow yourself a little gluttony and try Toledo's most typical candy—marzipan, full of the aroma of Spain.

Toledo: left, view of the Alcazar and the Tagus; above, the house of El Greco and, right, the Synagogue, one of the most beautiful in the world.

SALAMANCA, SALAMANCA...

Salamanca, Salamanca,
Renaciente maravilla.

Thus wrote Miguel de Unamuno (1864-1936) one of the most outstanding Spanish writers and philosophers. He taught Greek language and literature at the University of Salamanca for many years, then became its president and stayed there until his death.

The university of the ancient Castilian city was the focal point of the humanistic culture and the philosophical, spiritual and religious thought of Spain from the Middle Ages up to the Renaissance, thanks to the scholars who wrote works on all the fields of human knowledge and produced excellent translations from the Arabic at the behest of Alphonso the Wise. However, we now regard Salamanca with the eye rather of a wandering tourist than of a scholar.

So let us put our hands in our pockets and take an enquiring stroll around this lovely city, which rises like an amphitheater up the slopes of three hills along the banks of the Tormes, a tributary of the Duero. Here one is gripped by the mysterious fascination of the distant past, for Salamanca has retained its mediaeval shape almost unchanged. So let us make the tour of the *paseos,* avenues which follow the site of the ancient fortifications. We arrive in the center of the city, in the impressive Plaza Mayor which is surrounded by spacious colonnades, almost as if to isolate and protect it. Salamanca is crossed by two roads, one of which leads out of the city to the Paseo de la Glorieta, the other to the new bridge over the river. But we prefer to linger on the old bridge, the impressive Roman one rebuilt under the Emperor Trajan. It is 400 meters long and has 27 arches. From here we can pass through Arrabal del Puente, a suburb of Salamanca, and re-enter the city to take a closer look.

The Cathedral is at the top of most tourists' lists of sights to visit. In fact there are two of them, the Old and the New, and one goes to see them not only or so much, out of a sense of spiritual duty as because they offer the principal contact with the past and present thoughts and feelings of the inhabitants of Salamanca. The cathedral is one of those typical monuments in which one can clearly see the variety of architectural styles used over the two centuries or so in which the building went on, from 1513 to about 1733. The decoration of the portals and spires is Plateresque (a style rich in ornamentation, like that of a *platero* or silversmith), whilst the two domes are seventeenth century. The most striking feature is the fanciful and otiose decoration of the sculptures, examples of the so-called *churrigueresco,* a form of the Baroque developed by José Churriguera and his sons, who worked from the end of the seventeenth century to the end of the eighteenth. In other churches one can see often intermingled Gothic, Mozarabic and Byzantine styles and Roman sculptures, paintings and enamals, in a kind of kaleidoscopic arrangement which brings contrasting elements together without causing discordance.

The tower built in 1400 by Sotomayor is of interest, so is the House of the Shells, built in 1512 in a pure Isabelline style with a fine courtyard, a large tympanum over the doorway in the façade and the shapes of 300 cockleshells decorating the exterior walls.

Above: Salamanca, on the banks of the Rio Tormes. Left: the portal of the University, in the plateresque style; right, the Casa de las Conchas.

A SEASHELL AND A SHRINE

Any French gourmet will tell you that *coquilles St. Jacques* are an exquisite dish prepared from scallops. Scientists call this mollusc *Pecten Jacobeus-Linné,* but in the Middle Ages it meant one thing: pilgrimage.

St. James (St. Jacques in French and Santiago in Spanish) was one of the twelve apostles. He was martyred in Palestine, and there is a tradition that his relics were brought in a tiny unmanned ship to the tip of Galicia in Spain in the first century A.D. The ship landed close to the little village of Compostela. Thus St. James returned to Spain, where he had once preached the Gospel.

Several centuries later in 813 the burial-place of the apostle was re-discovered. Soon afterwards were in great danger of losing a battle against the Moors, and suddenly St. Jacques appeared and led them to victory.

Above the tiny, ancient shrine they built one of the most magnificent and interesting churches in Spain, showing the influence of French and Lombardian culture because of the many pilgrims coming to Compostela from those parts. In fact the miracle attracted pilgrims from all over Europe who came to atone for their sins of offer a gift for favors received, inspired by faith or less noble motives. All pilgrims wore the **compostelas,** pieces of parchment which bore a seal affixed in the Chapel of the Kings of France at the end of their pilgrimage. They carried a pilgrim's staff with a gourd of water attached and wore a flowing cape of heavy material. They had stout sandals on their feet and wore a felt hat with the brim turned up at the front and adorned with a scallop shell, the symbol of another miracle. This miracle happened when one day a young man was riding along the shore on his wedding. He suddenly fell into the sea and disappeared. St. James was called on for help, and not in vain, for the young bridegroom soon emerged from the waves covered in scallop shells. That is how *Pecten Jacobeus-Linné* became the symbol of Christian pilgrimage, and even today in certain parts of Europe "to take the scallop shell" means going on a pilgrimage.

In those days a long road bristling with difficulties made this journey, usually done on foot, a very arduous one. For weeks and weeks the pilgrims toiled across barren uplands, through mountain passes like Roncesvalles and Somport, over the Pyrenees through rivers and over fords, in danger from bandits, sickness and hardships of all kinds. Nevertheless thousands upon thousands of people set off for Compostela, including Charlemagne, many kings, queens and famous men such as St. Ignatius Loyola.

Today it is possible to get to Compostela in a very short time indeed. Santiago de Compostela still retains its prestige and attraction, thanks to its university and fine churches and monasteries. But visitors must still enter St. James's shrine with a humble pilgrim's heart. As tradition demands, the pilgrim must embrace his statue behind the altar and acquire wisdom by knocking his head against the image of Mateo, the sculptor who carved the *Portico de la Gloria* with its smiling figure of the prophet Daniel.

There is a story that Daniel is smiling because opposite him is the statue of Queen Esther, said by one bygone cardinal to be much too beautiful. But if beauty is a gift from God, what is wrong with Daniel's innocent admiration?

Santiago de Compostela, one of the most popular shrines in medieval Europe, its cathedral and the picturesque stairs nearby seen in the late afternoon light.

THE CITY ON THE "GREAT RIVER"

Guadalquivir, a Spanish name derived from the Arabic *Wadi el Kebir,* means "Great River". On the left bank of this river the Phoenicians built Cordoba, which in the course of centuries came under the domination of the Romans, Byzantines and Goths until it finally became a symbol of Moorish power in Spain. In the year 711 the Arabs crossed the Straits of Gibraltar in a lightning campaign and conquered the Iberian peninsula. They made Cordoba their capital, and it soon became the cultural pivot of Europe and the meeting-place of artists, doctors, astronomers and scholars of many nations. Equally important were craftsman of Cordoba, who worked in 80,000 shops or workshops. Cordoban leatherwork techniques for turning goastskins into superb bags, purses and footwear, became a byword for excellent quality.

Moreover the caliphs of Cordoba made the city one of the most important centers of the Islamic faith. Every day from the many minarets which pointed to the skies, the muezzins of Cordoba called the faithful to prayer in its 500 or so mosques, the largest of which was considered the finest in the world and only slightly smaller than the Great Mosque at Mecca.

In 1236, when the Christians reconquered Cordoba, the Arabs moved their capital to Granada, where it remained for the next 250 years. The new masters of Cordoba built their church in the middle of the mosque erected several centuries earlier by Abd al Rahman and enlarged and embellished by later caliphs. This is an interesting contrast with later Spanish practice, when Cortez and Pizzaro plundered and demolished Aztec and Inca temples in Mexico and Peru to put up Christian cathedrals which proved all too often superfluous. This mosque-cum-cathedral is of immense interest because it clearly shows the wide range of architectural influences at work, from Roman and Syrian art to Gothic and plateresque, from the Byzantine splendor of the mosaics to the ribbing of the dome showing Persian influence and the nave with its crossed arches supported by 800 columns. In the center of the mosque is the cathedral with its Renaissance transept in the plateresque style.

In many churches, chapels and porches one can see examples of the *mudéjar* style which continued the Moorish tradition even after the Christians had reconquered large areas of Spain under Ferdinand III, king and saint.

In Cordoba everything still speaks eloquently of long-dead Arabs who loved this place deeply. Their memory lives on in the ancient Synagogue, the houses, the flower-laden balconies and in certain narrow white streets which sometimes offer a glimpse of the remains of an ancient miranet and give one the illusion of being in an Arab city. The memory of the Moorish period also lives on in the words for certain everyday objects and in the use of spices such as saffron and pepper in many dishes. The monument to the famous bullfighter Manolete is a true expression of Spanish popular taste and feeling.

Cordova. Above: the Roman bridge and the interior of the famous Mosque with its forest of columns and the cupola of the *mirhab*.

ALLAH STILL WATCHES OVER THE ALHAMBRA

"Allah still watches over the Alhambra" the Spaniards say of the marvellous *Al Qa'a al Hamra* ("the Red Castle"), built in the thirteenth and fourteenth centuries on a hilltop in Granada in southern Spain. For the fact that we can still enjoy this jewel of Moorish art we have Washington Irving, not Allah, to thank. Despite its desolation and decay he found the place so fascinating that he spent much of 1829 there writing his "Tales of the Alhambra". The interest aroused by the book gave the deserted palace so much publicity that the authorities decided to do the restoration work needed to save a treasure which is widely agreed to be part of the artistic heritage of the whole world.

The Alhambra stands on its hilltop, in the valley below lies the wonderful city of Granada (the name means "pomegranate"), in the background rise the snowy mountains of the Sierra Nevada.

The predominant color of the Alhambra is rust-red, from the large amounts of local clay which went into its construction. It is not a single building but a group of towers and palaces built over several centuries during the period of Moorish domination and preserved by Ferdinand of Aragon and Isabella of Castille when they finally defeated the Moors in 1492 after a long struggle and took possession of the city.

The Alhambra represents the best and richest example of Moorish art, as witness its lacy stonework, fine many-colored majolica tiles, wood filigrees and delicately-tinted stucco decorations framing verses in Arabic script, the Hall of the Ambassadors, the throne with its lofty cupola and the seven Heavens of Islam inlaid in the ceiling, the splendid Court of the Myrtles, 130 feet long, paved with white marble and named after the myrtle hedges which surround the pool in the center.

The Court of the Lions, in the palace of the same name, is another masterpiece: twelve standing lions sculptured in grey Greek marble and grouped around an alabaster fountain. It is connected with the Hall of the Abencerrajes, a Granadan family whose fortunes and misfortunes were set to music by the Italian composer Luigi Cherubini.

The Gardens of the Generalife, the Summer Palace of the kings of Granada (in Arabic *Jennal al Arif* means "Garden of the Architect") are wonderful. They contain rows of cypresses, arcades of box-trees, orange-trees, jasmine, almond-trees and roses which fill the air with heady perfume. These gardens inspired Manuel de Falla to write his symphonic impressions under the title *Noches en los jardines de España.*

Water is another great attraction: it spurts up in the *Patio de los Surtidores,* gushes down the great stone steps and gurgles in the many fountains.

Of all the many precious heirlooms left by the Arabs in this land they ruled for so many centuries, one can never be overrated: the irrigation system. This has remained almost unchanged to this very day. In fact the Arabs' water systems, changing the course of the River Dauro, enabled them to transform the barren hill near Granada into a sea of greenery.

Granada, at the foot of the Sierra Nevada, and the Alhambra—the most impressive of all the architectural remains left by the Arabs in Spain.

BY THE ALCAZAR OF SEVILLE

When Bizet's fiery Carmen sings her famous song about the delights of drinking wine and dancing the *seguidilla* by the Alcazar of Seville she is expressing something of the real spirit of Andalusia, one aspect of a Spanish region rich in contrasts and marvels.

Seville, the capital of Andalusia, is like Cordoba in having Iberian or Phoenician origins. Of its many rulers the most important were the Arabs. Built along the banks of the Guadalquivir, Seville, though far from the sea, has a port which can accomodate ships of fairly large tonnage.

To understand and get to know Seville one must walk along the street which skirts the river benenath the blossoming trees, through shops and cafés, through the *barrios* of Santa Cruz, la Sierpes and Triana, which are the real

and colorful heart of the city. An important landmark is the superb cathedral, the largest Gothic church in the world. Built in 1401 on the site of a former mosque, it is rich in works of art, including paintings by Goya, Zurbarán and Murillo, the latter being buried in the ancient Jewish quarter. There are fine sculptures in marble and alabaster and the tomb of Christopher Columbus. He assembled his expedition in Seville in 1492 and returned there following year at the end of his first voyage. The Florentine Amerigo Vespucci also set off from Seville for the New World.

The tower of the Giralda, which stands next to the cathedral, is 305 feet high and the pride and joy of the Sevillians. Its rosy walls, 43 feet wide and 8 feet thick, hark back to the twelfth century miranet turned into a bell-tower in 1395.

The magic of Seville. Left: a typical house. Below, the Golden Tower, on the banks of the Guadalquivir; right, the Giralda and the Plaza de España.

There are so many things to admire here. The *Patio de los Naranjos* ("Court of the Orange Trees"), the Alcazar where lovers stroll as once did Charles V and Isabella of Portugal, the *Torre del Oro* ("Tower of Gold"), the Gothic churches built to replace ancient mosques, the palaces decorated with *azulejos* (typical majolica tiles), the *Fabrica de Tabacos,* the *Arena de la Maestranza,* the excellent Museum and the Hospital of the Caridad, founded by Don Juan Tenorio of immortal musical and literary fame.

One of the best times to visit Seville is that of the *fiestas.* These can be subdivided into *ferias* (fairs), *romerías* (pilgrimages), *verbenas* (patronal feastdays) and Holy Week processions. The *fiestas* continue traditions going back a thousand years. They always include balls, concerts with regional music and colorful local costumes, decorations and bullfights.

COIMBRA IN PORTUGAL

Songs and candies have been named after it, its praises have been sung in so many ways, and indeed Coimbra is one of the most fascinating of Portuguese cities. It stands in an enchanting position on the left bank of the River Mondego half way up the Sierra del Lavrao.

Coimbra has two faces. one face is that of a modern industrial town which does a brisk trade in linen, ceramics, vegetables and good wine. The other is old, even ancient. The origins of Coimbra go back to the period of Roman rule, when the city was called Eminium. Than came the domination of the Visigoths, and in the seventh century under the name of Coimbriga it was so important as a commercial center that the four kings who ruled from 561 to 640 A.D. had their own stud-farms there. In their turn the Arabs took over the city and built massive fortifications around it, which did not prevent the Christians under Alfonso of Leon from recapturing it, only to lose it to the Arabs once again. Ferdinand the Great conquered the city for good, and when Portugal became an independent kingdom Coimbra was chosen as its capital.

There are many interesting cultural monuments to tell us of Coimbra's complicated past. The most important is beyond doubt the fine Romanesque cathedral of *Se'Velha*, whose design reminds one strongly of Santiago de Compostella. The Church of Santa Cruz, in the Manueline style, was built between 1517 and 1521 by French

architects brought to Portugal by King Manuel. Of particular interest are the sculptured pulpits and two important tombs built for the founders of the Portuguese monarchy, Alfonso Henriquez (1185) and his son Sancho, who died in 1211.

The Italian Renaissance style introduced by the famous sculptor and architect Sansovino, who lived in Portugal between 1490 and 1499, has left its mark in many places: in the Porta Speciosa of the cathedral (much eroded because of the softness of the stone), in the lovely doorway (now in the local museum) from the former Convent of St. Thomas and in the Chapel of the Blessed Sacrament, built in 1566.

Another richly-decorated church is that of St. Bento, attributed to the Italian Filippo Terzi, along with the Cloisters of the Misericordia and the city's aqueduct, still working well today. Very interesting is the Bishop's Palace, now the Museo Machaco de Castro, which contains antiquities, ceramics, silver and ivory. There are impressive Botanical Gardens, created by the Italian Domenico Vandelli in 1774. But the feature which made Coimbra the center of literary, artistic and scientific activity in Portugal was the university, founded in 1290 and until 1911 the only one in the country.

The University of Coimbra (Portugal), one of the most famous cultural centers in Old Europe. Opposite page, the main portal; above, an inner courtyard and, left, the door to the library.

NAVIGARE NECESSE EST

Curiosity drives mankind to seek out the reason for events, to discover what lies beyond the next bend in the road or what is concealed in the hearts of others. It is a magic device which enables one to make progress, improve the world and help oneself and others. Curiosity is the basis of all discovery and invention. If Newton had not tried to find out why the apple fell and Galileo had not investigated why the lamp in the cathedral of Pisa was swinging, if Fleming had thrown away his cultures instead of wondering why they were showing traces of mold, how humanity's progress would have been held back! But luckily for us every century has had its men of curiosity, some of whom were not content with the privileged ease in which they lived and chose to abandon comfort and riches in search of an answer to their questions.

Henry, son of John I of Portugal, born in Oporto at the end of the fourteenth century, was one of these extraordinary men. Trained in the harsh arts of war, he soon showed that he deserved his father's trust and esteem. When only twenty the young prince won his spurs in 1415 for his valor at the capture of the fortress of Ceuta on the coast of Africa opposite Gibraltar. This was the enterprise which brought the prince to Africa and, according to the chronicles, fanned young Henry's desire to see "what there was below the Canary Islands."

On his return to Portugal he founded the city of Tercena Naval (nowadays Sagres) where he settled down in a castle named the *Villa do Infante* after him, and set up a center for seamanship and sea-lore. But his stay in Portugal was always brief, for the thin, pale prince spent most of his time organising new expeditions. His Portuguese and Italian captains sailed from Tercena and won fame for themselves in various enterprises.

One of his prime objectives was to round Cape Bojador, which until then had been achieved only by Genoese sailors around the mid-thirteenth century. It was a particularly difficult area because of adverse currents, strong winds, superstitions which paralysed the sailors with fear and made them refuse to embark. They were convinced that the Atlantic was the home of sea-monsters.

Henry was tenacious and overcame all resistance. After his first success came the great discoveries, the Rio de Oro, Cape Blanc, Cape Verdi and Senegal, to mention only a few, as well as his expeditions into the African interior. But Henry was not content to turn the prows of his ships towards unknown shores. Every inch a humanist, he founded chairs of theology, mathematics and medicine at the University of Lisbon and particularly encouraged the study of cartography. His life was also devoted to the discovery of new sea-routes which could break the Arabo-Venetian hegemony of the spice trade. In his castle experts in navigation, cartographers and astronomers thoroughly trained the men who were to embark on the royal vessels and win Portugal one of the largest colonial empires in the world. And one day Lisbon immortalised them with a magnificient monument to their memory.

Unforgettable Lisbon. A short distance from the statue of Henry the Navigator (left and right), the Tower of Belem, on the bank of the Tagus, past which the fleets sponsored by this adventurous prince once sailed. Last page: the famous Dancing Faun (Pompei).

Credits : Aotany/Atlas : 21c — Arboit/End Papers : 56b, 58a, c, 59a, b, c — Bartel/Vloo : 1 — Bauer/Bavaria : 32b — Bavaria-Verlag : 36a, b, 37b, c, 64 — Benser/Zefa : 25 — Berne/Fotogram : 20a, 21a, b, 38a, b, 60b — Bertot/Atlas : 5 — Bochet/Vloo : 26a — Boehn/Fotogram : 26b — Bohnacker/Bavaria : 71a — Bonnotte/Atlas : 88a, 89 — Boutié/Atlas : 78a, 79a — Buga : 55a — Buga/Unedi : 66 — Cabaud/Fotogram : 53b — Cérard/Fotogram : 78b — Corson/Fotogram : End Papers — Damm/Zefa : 46a — Deckart/Zefa : 33 — Driver/Fotogram : 21d — Errath/Explorer : 6 — Fiore : 4, 5, 18, 51, 68, 75a — Froissardey/Atlas : 87a — Gaetano/Bavaria : 60a — Galdiger/Tourisme suisse : 43a — Garbison/Fotogram : 49 — Gauroy/Atlas : 62a — Gerster : 67, 69a, b — Giegel/OFST : 44a, b — Giger/Tourisme suisse : 42a, b — Goebel/Zefa : 47 — Goldner/Atlas : 22b — Gollow/Zefa : 24a, b — Grossauer/Zefa : 41a — Guillou/Atlas : 35, 82a, 86a — Günert/OFVW : 40c — Hädeler/Bavaria : 12b — Henneghien/ Fotogram : 63a — Hetz/Zefa : 30b — Hille/Zefa : 37a — Hureau/Atlas : 94a — I.IA.G : 48a, 50b, 69a — Kanus/Atlas : 10 — Kanus/Bavaria : 8b — Kerth/Zefa : 76b, 93b — de Laubier/Pix : 2a, b, 3a, b, c — Lenars/Atlas : 14a, b, 87b — Len Sirman : 54a — Leprohon : 20b, 45a, 54b, 55b, 76b — Loucel/Fotogram : 22a, 23 — Lüthi/Bavaria : 95 — Mangez/Vloo : 16a — Markowitsch/OT : 40b — Marzari : 61 — Mathey/Vloo : 79b — Messerschmidt/Bavaria : 29a, c, 94b — Mistler/Vloo : 16b — Nauta : 85b, 86b — Office du Tourisme autrichien : 39a — Office du Tourisme espagnol : 81b — Omnia/Bavaria : 30a, 31 — Pedone : 70a — Petit/Atlas : 82b, 93a — Phillips/Zefa : 12a — Picou/ Fotogram : 15 — Pizzi/Gemini : 8a, 9b, 10b, 11b, 19a, 28b, 32c, 50a, 52a, b, 53a, 56a, 58b, 60b, 74a, 75b, 77, 80, 81a, 83, 84, 85a, 88b, 90b, 91a, b, 92, 96 — Pr/Ricciarini : 39b — Prädel/Zefa : 17b, 46b — Puck/Bavaria : 34, 43b — Quinsard/Atlas : 70b, 71c — Salou/Atlas : 27 — Sammer/Bavaria : 28a — Schmidt/Bavaria : 29b — Schmied/Bavaria : 45b — Scholtz/Bavaria : 32a — STR/Bavaria : 48b — Sturm/Bavaria : 90a — Thiele/Bavaria : 76a — Tondew/Atlas : 72 — Unedi : 63b, 69c — Viollet : 65, 71b, 73a, b — Warwicks/Allan Cash : 9a — Watteau/Vloo : 17a — Williams/Vloo : 7 — Wolfsberger/Zefa : 40a — Zeitbild/Bavaria : 57.

Designed and Produced
by Productions Liber S.A.   © Productions Liber S.A., Fribourg, 1982   ISBN 0-517-356163

Achevé d'imprimer par Sagdos,
Brugherio-Milan, le 20 Mars 1982
Printed in Italy